AF541773

CORPORATE PERFORMANCE AND GOVERNANCE

CORPORATE PERFORMANCE AND GOVERNANCE

Edited by

Dr. Suman Kalyan Chaudhury

M.Com, MBA, PGDPM & IR, LLB, Ph.D.

Reader cum Placement Officer

P.G. Department of Business Administration

Berhampur University

Berhampur

(Odisha)

DISCOVERY PUBLISHING HOUSE PVT. LTD.

NEW DELHI-110 002

Published by:
Tilak Wasan

DISCOVERY PUBLISHING HOUSE PVT. LTD.
4383/4A, Ansari Road, Darya Ganj
New Delhi-110 002 (India)
Phone : +91-11-23279245, 43596064-65
Fax : +91-11-23253475
E-mail : parul.wasan@gmail.com
discoverypublishinghouse@gmail.com
web : www.discoverypublishinggroup.com

***First Edition:* 2012**
ISBN: 978-93-5056-052-5

Corporate Performance and Governance

Printed at:
Shree Balaji Art Press
Delhi

Preface

The concept of corporate governance, which emerged as a response to corporate failures and widespread dissatisfaction with the way many corporate function, has become one of the wide and deep discussions across the globe recently. It primarily hinges on complete transparency, integrity and accountability of the management. There is also an increasingly greater focus on investor protection and public interest. Corporate Governance is concerned with the values, vision and visibility. It is about the value orientation of the organization, ethical norms for its performance, the direction of development and social accomplishment of the organization and the visibility of its performance and practices.

Corporate Governance has assumed vital role and significance due to globalization and liberalization. With the opening of economy and to be in line with WTO requirements, if the Indian corporate have to survive and succeed amidst increasing competition globally, it can only be through transparency in operations. The excellence in terms of customer satisfaction, in terms of return, in terms of product and service, in terms of return to promoters and in terms of social responsibilities towards society and people cannot be achieved without practising good Corporate Governance.

In this book an attempt is made to highlight the main areas where there exist loopholes in the prevailing system, suggestive measures to make the corporate governance system effective and efficient. It is hoped that the book will be usefull to researchers, shareholders, corporate, governments, banks and academicians.

Dr. Suman Kalyan Chaudhury

Acknowledgement

Every action requires an initiator, influencer. I am initiated into writing this book, primarily, by the inspiration provided by my students and friends in the same profession. My colleagues are always stand with for support and cheering me. Therefore, I can't but gratefully acknowledge my indebtedness to all those who have extended generous assistance in the successful accomplishment of this indispensable work. It will be a serious blunder if I forget to mention some of my colleagues Prof. Niranjan Nayak, Center Head, Koustav Business School; Dr. Kirti Ranjan Swain, Associate Prof., IPSAR Business School, Cuttack; Dr. Ashok Kumar Panigrahi, Asst. Prof, RITEE Business School, Raipur; Prof. Ashok Kumar Panda, Dean, Astha School of Management for their ardent encouragement and beacon guidance in bringing out this work.

I profusely thank my chairman of the institute, Er. Sundhansu Kumar Dash for his rock support and continuous push that furthered my efforts seamlessly towards quick accomplishment. My heartfelt gratitude to him.

Last but not least my heartfelt gratitude to my wife sinu knows no bounds for her immaculate co-operation. Needless to depict, I am indebted to my family members for their love which affection and inspired me in my problem solving while in action.

I am also much beholden to Mr. Tilak Wasan, Managing Director, Discovery Publishing House Pvt. Ltd., New Delhi for publishing the work in a record time.

Dr. Suman Kalyan Chaudhury

Contents

Preface
Acknowledgement
Contributors

1. Role of Corporate Governance in Development of Co-operative Banks in India 1
Dr. Aravind.S; Dr. Santosh Singh Bais

2. Corporate Governance in India: Lessons and Actions 15
Dr. Ashok Kumar Panigrahi

3. Corporate Governance in Banks 33
Ms. Vimla Virparia

4. Corporate Governance in Indian Financial Institutions: Theories and Practices 45
Prof. Sanjay Kanti Das

5. Non-Banking Financial Companies Tragedy of Economic History of Modern India 109
Dr. K. S. Vataliya; Mr. H. D. Vyas

6. Prudential Way of Tapping Global Opportunities by Indian Companies 116
Mr. Giridhari Mohanta; Dr. Snehalkumar H Mistry

7. Corporate Governance in Banks 128
Dr. Santosh Singh Bais, Mr. Srinivas Ranoor

8. Role of Independent Directors in Good Corporate Governance In India 138
Prof. Trilok Nath Shukla; Prof. Chumki Chatterjee

9. Corporate Governance Agenda of New Millennium With Special Reference to Banking Sector 168
Dr. Jagannath B. kukkudi
Prof. Nagaratna M. Chowdhary

10. An Analysis of Models/Mechanisms in Corporate Governance 179
Dr. Aravind.S.; Dr. Fisseha Girma Tessema
Dr. Hailay Gebretinsae

Index 195

Contributors

1 **Dr. Ashok Kumar Panigrahi,** Associate Professor, Dept. of Commerce and Management, REET School of Management, Raipur, Chhattisgarh.

2 **Dr. Arvinda S, Professor,** Department, of Management, College of Business and Economics, Adi-Haqi Campus, Mekelle University, P.O. Box: 451, Mekelle, Tigray, Ethiopia.

3 **Dr. Suman Kalyan Chaudhury**, M.Com, MBA, PGDPM & IR, Ph.D., Reader cum Placement Officer, Department of MBA., Berhampur University, Berhampur, (Odisha).

4 **Dr. Jagdish. R. Raiyani,** Assistant Prof, Faculty of Management, Shree Maharshi Dayanand Saraswati MBA College, Tankara, Rajkot, Gujarat.

5 **Dr. Santosh Singh Bais**, Assistant Professor, Department of Commerce and Management Government, First Grade College, Chincholi, Karnataka.

6 **Ms. Vimla Virparia,** Assistant Prof., Narmada College of Management, Bharuch, Gujurat.

7 **Prof. Sanjay Kanti Das,** Asstt. Professor, Commerce, Lumding College, Lumding, Nagaon, Assam.

8 **Dr. Sudhansu Kumar Das**, Lecturer in Commerce, V.N (Auto) College, Jajpur Road, Odisha.

9 **Dr. K.S. Vataliya,** Assistant Professor, Dept. of Commerce and Management, Govt. First Grade College Chincholi, Karnataka.

10 **Mr. H.D. Vyas,** Assistant Professor, Department of Commerce and Management, Govt. First Grade College Chincholi, Karnataka.

11 **Prof. Trilok Nath Shukla,** Sr. Lecturer, Bharatiya Vidya Bhavan, Bhubaneswar, Odisha.

12 **Prof. Chumuki Chatarjee,** Lecture, Bharatiya Vidya Bhavan,Bhubaneswar,Odisha.

13 **Mr. Giridhari Mohanta,** Lecturer, Rajdhani College of Engineering and Management, Bhubaneswar, Odisha.

14 **Dr. Snehalkumar H Mistry,** Assistant Professor, C.K. Pithawalla Institute of Management, Surat, Gujurat.

15 **Dr. Jagannath B. kukkudi** Assistant Professor, Govt. First Grade College Kalagi, Tq: Chittapur Dist: Gulbarga, Karnataka.

16 **Prof. Nagaratna M. Chowdhary**, Guest Lecturer and Research Scholar, Government First Grade College Gulbarga, Karnataka.

17 **Dr. Fisseha Girma Tessema,** Assistant Professor, Department of Accounting and Finance, College of Business and Economics, Mekelle University, Mekelle, Ethiopia.

18 **Dr. Hailay Gebretinsae,** Head and Assistant Professor, Department of Management, College of Business and Economics, Mekelle University, Mekelle, Ethiopia.

1

Role of Corporate Governance in Development of Co-operative Banks in India

Dr. Aravind S

Dr. Santosh Singh Bais

ABSTRACT

Corporate governance especially in the co-operative sector has come into sharp focus because more and more co-operative banks in India, both in urban and rural areas, have experienced grave problems in recent times which has in a way threatened the profile and identity of the entire cooperative system. These problems include mis-management, financial impropriety, poor investment decisions and the growing distance between members and their co-operative society.

The purpose and objectives of co-operatives provide the framework for co-operative corporate governance. Co-operatives are organized groups of people and jointly managed and democratically controlled enterprises. They exist to serve their members and depositors and produce benefits for them. Co-operative corporate governance is therefore about ensuring co-operative relevance and performance by connecting members, management and the employees to the policy, strategy and decision-making processes.

In the years to come, the Indian financial system will grow not only in size but also in complexity as the forces of competition gain further momentum and financial markets acquire greater depth. We can assure you that the policy environment will remain supportive of healthy growth and development with accent on more operational flexibility as well as greater prudential regulation and supervision. The real success of our financial sector reforms will however depend primarily on the organizational effectiveness of the banks, including cooperative banks, for which initiatives will have to come from the banks themselves. It is for the co-operative banks themselves to build on the synergy inherent in the cooperative structure and stand up for their unique qualities. With elements of good corporate governance, sound investment policy, appropriate internal control systems, better credit risk management, focus on newly-emerging business areas like micro finance, commitment to better customer service, adequate automation and proactive policies on house-keeping issues, co-operative banks will definitely be able to grapple with these challenges and convert them into opportunities.

Introduction

For the co-operative banks in India, these are challenging times. Never before has the need for restoring customer confidence in the cooperative sector been felt so much. Never before has the issue of good governance in the co-operative banks assumed such criticality. The literature on corporate governance in its wider connotation covers a range of issues such as protection of shareholders' rights, enhancing shareholders' value, Board issues including its composition and role, disclosure requirements, integrity of accounting practices, the control systems, in particular internal control systems.

Corporate governance especially in the co-operative sector has come into sharp focus because more and more co-operative banks in India, both in urban and rural areas, have experienced grave problems in recent times which has in a way threatened the profile and identity of the entire cooperative system. These problems include mismanagement, financial impropriety, poor investment decisions and the growing distance between members and their co-operative society. The purpose and objectives of co-operatives provide the framework for co-operative corporate governance. Co-operatives are organized groups of people and jointly managed and democratically controlled enterprises. They exist to serve their members and depositors and produce benefits for them. Co-operative corporate governance is therefore about ensuring co-operative relevance and performance by connecting members, management and the employees to the policy, strategy and decision-making processes.

Genesis of Corporate Governance

The seeds of modern corporate governance were probably sown by the Watergate scandal in the USA. Subsequent investigations by US regulatory and legislative bodies highlighted control failures that had allowed several major corporations to make illegal political contributions and bribe government officials. While these developments in the US stimulated debate in the UK, a spate of scandals and collapses in that country in the late 1980s and early 1990s led shareholders and banks to worry about their investments. Several companies in UK which saw explosive growth in earnings in the 80s ended the decade in a memorably disastrous manner. Importantly, such spectacular corporate failures arose primarily out of poorly managed business practices.

This debate was driven partly by the subsequent enquiries into corporate governance (most notably the Cadbury Report) and partly by extensive changes in corporate structure. In May 1991, the London Stock Exchange set up a Committee under the chairmanship of Sir Arian Cadbury to help raise the standards of corporate governance and the level of confidence in financial reporting and auditing by setting out clearly what it sees as the respective responsibilities of those involved and what it believes is expected of them. The Committee investigated accountability of the Board of Directors to shareholders and to the society. It submitted its report and the associated *'Code of Best Practices'* in December 1992 wherein it spelt out the methods of governance needed to achieve a balance between the essential powers of the Board of Directors and their proper accountability. Being a pioneering report on corporate governance, it would perhaps be in order to make a brief reference to its recommendations which are in the nature of guidelines relating to, among other things, the Board of Directors and Reporting & Control.

The Cadbury Report stipulated that the Board of Directors should meet regularly, retain full and effective control over the company and monitor the executive management. There should be a clearly accepted division of responsibilities at the head of the company which will ensure balance of power and authority so that no individual has unfettered powers of decision. The Board should have a formal schedule of matters specifically reserved to it for decisions to ensure that the direction and control of the company is firmly in its hands. There should also be an agreed procedure for Directors in the furtherance of their duties to take independent professional advice.

The Cadbury Report generated a lot of interest in India. The issue of corporate governance was studied in depth and dealt with by the Confederation of Indian Industries (CII), Associated Chamber of Commerce and Industry (ASSOCHAM) and Securities and Exchange Board of India (SEBI). These studies reinforced the Cadbury Report's focus on the crucial role of the Board and the need for it to observe a Code of Best Practices. Co-operative banks as corporate entities possess certain unique characteristics. Paradoxical as it may sound, evolution of co-operatives in India as peoples' organizations rather than business enterprises adopting professional managerial systems has hindered growth of professionalism in co-operatives and proved to be a neglected area in their evolution.

The Special Place of Banking

The banking sector is not necessarily totally corporate. Some part of it is, of course, but a segment of banks is mostly government owned as statutory corporations or run as cooperatives—just like your bank. Banking as a sector has been unique and the interests of other stakeholders appear more important to it than in the case of non-banking and non-finance organizations. In the case of traditional manufacturing corporations, the issue has been that of safeguarding and maximizing the shareholders' value. In the case of banking, the risk involved for depositors and the possibility of contagion assumes greater importance than that of consumers of manufactured products. Further, the involvement of government is discernibly higher in banks due to importance of stability of financial system and the larger interests of the public. Since the market control is not sufficient to ensure proper governance in banks, the government does see reason in regulating and controlling the nature of activities, the structure of bonds, the ownership pattern, capital adequacy norms, liquidity ratios, etc.

Reasons for High Degree of Oversight

There are three reasons for degree of government oversight in this sector:

- Firstly, it is believed that the depositors, particularly retail depositors, can not effectively protect themselves as they do not have adequate information, nor are they in a position to coordinate with each other.
- Secondly, bank assets are unusually opaque, and lack transparency as well as liquidity. This condition arises due to the fact that most bank loans, unlike other products and services, are usually customized and privately negotiated.
- Thirdly, it is believed that there could be a contagion effect resulting from the instability of one bank, which would affect a class of banks or even the entire financial system and the economy. As one bank becomes unstable,

there may be a heightened perception of risk among depositors for the entire class of such banks, resulting in a run on the deposits and putting the entire financial system in jeopardy.

Role of the Government and the Regulator

Regulators are external pressure points for good corporate governance. Mere compliance with regulatory requirements is not however an ideal situation in itself. In fact, mere compliance with regulatory pressures is a minimum requirement of good corporate governance and what are required are internal pressures, peer pressures and market pressures to reach higher than minimum standards prescribed by regulatory agencies. RBI's approach to regulation in recent times has some features that would enhance the need for and usefulness of good corporate governance in the co-operative sector. The transparency aspect has been emphasized by expanding the coverage of information and timeliness of such information and analytical content. Importantly, deregulation and operational freedom must go hand in hand with operational transparency. In fact, the RBI has made it clear that with the abolition of minimum lending rates for co-operative banks, it will be incumbent on these banks to make the interest rates charged by them transparent and known to all customers. Banks have therefore been asked to publish the minimum and maximum interest rates charged by them and display this information in every branch. Disclosure and transparency are thus key pillars of a corporate governance framework because they provide all the stakeholders with the information necessary to judge whether their interests are being taken care of. We in RBI see transparency and disclosure as an important adjunct to the supervisory process as they facilitate market discipline of banks.

Another area which requires focused attention is greater transparency in the balance sheets of co-operative banks. The commercial banks in India are now required to disclose accounting ratios relating to operating profit, return on assets, business per employee, NPAs, etc. as also maturity profile of loans, advances, investments, borrowings and deposits. The issue before us now is how to adapt similar disclosures suitably to be captured in the audit reports of co-operative banks. RBI had advised Registrars of Co-operative Societies of the state governments in 1996 that the balance sheet and profit & loss account should be prepared based on prudential norms introduced as a sequel to Financial Sector Reforms and that the statutory/departmental auditors of co-operative banks should look into the compliance with these norms. Auditors are therefore expected to be well-versed with all aspects of the new guidelines issued by RBI and ensure that the profit & loss account and balance sheet of cooperative banks are prepared in a transparent manner and reflect the true state of affairs. Auditors should also ensure that other necessary statutory provisions and appropriations out of profits are made as required in terms of the Co-operative Societies Act / Rules of the state concerned and the bye-laws of the respective institutions.

Board of Director and their Committees

At the initiative of the RBI, a consultative group, aimed at strengthening corporate governance in banks, headed by Dr. Ashok Ganguli was set up to review the supervisory role of Board of banks. The recommendations include the role and responsibility of independent non-executive directors, qualification and other eligibility criteria for appointment of non-executive directors, training the directors and keeping them update with the latest developments. For private sector banks, etc. it is unanimously accepted that the most crucial aspect of corporate governance is that the organization have a professional board which can drive the organization through its ability to perform its responsibility of meeting regularly, retaining full and effective control over the company and monitor the executive management. Some of the important recommendations on the constitution of the Board are:

- Qualification and other eligibility criteria for appointment of non-executive directors.
- Defining role and responsibilities of directors including the recommended "Deed of Covenant" to be executed by the bank and the directors in conduct of the board functions.
- Training the directors and keeping them abreast of the latest developments.

Measures Taken by Banks Towards Implementation of Best Practices

1. *Prudential Norms*

Prudential norms in terms of income recognition, asset classification, and capital adequacy have been well assimilated by the Indian banking system. In keeping with the international best practice, starting 31st March 2004, banks have adopted 90 days norm for classification of NPAs. Also, norms governing provisioning requirements in respect of doubtful assets have been made more stringent in a phased manner. Beginning 2005, banks will be required to set aside capital charge for market risk on their trading portfolio of government investments, which was earlier virtually exempt from market risk requirement.

2. *Capital Adequacy*

All the Indian banks, barring one, today are well above the stipulated benchmark of 9 per cent and remain in a state of preparedness to achieve the best standards of CRAR as soon as the new Basel 2 norms are made operational. In fact, as of 31st March 2009, banking system as a whole had a CRAR close to 17 per cent.

3. *Income Recognition Front*

On the Income Recognition Front, there is complete uniformity now in the banking industry and the system therefore ensures responsibility and accountability on the part of the management in proper accounting of income as well as loan impairment.

4. ***ALM and Risk Management Practices***

At the initiative of the regulators, banks were quickly required to address the need for Asset Liability Management followed by risk management practices. Both these are critical areas for an effective oversight by the Board and the senior management which are implemented by the Indian banking system on a tight time frame and the implementation review by RBI. These steps have enabled banks to understand measure and anticipate the impact of the interest rate risk and liquidity risk, which in deregulated environment is gaining importance.

5. ***Professionalism***

Professionalism reflects the co-existence of high level of skills and standards in performing duties entrusted to an individual. The absence of a proper system of placement and skill up-gradation inputs constrain professional management in co-operative banks. Though there is a system of training in place in many co-operative banks, attempts are seldom made to match them with the current and future staff requirements. It is desirable that the training programs encompass skill up-gradation and aptitude development in full measure. It is also necessary to keep the staff sufficiently motivated through periodic job rotation, job enrichment and recognition of performance. The co-operative banks should indeed work like professional organizations on sound managerial systems in tune with the needs of the time taking care of future projections of requirements to retain and improve their market share and identity in the long run. It is in this context that professionalism and accountability of the banks' boards assume such critical significance.

6. ***Internal Control Systems***

Appropriate internal control systems become even more critical in the context of the growing emphasis on diversification of business products as the prime need at all levels in co-operative credit institutions. It is indeed necessary for co-operative banks to devote adequate attention to maximizing their returns on every unit of resources through an effective funds management strategy and mechanism.

7. *Development of Human Capital*

Success of economic decisions depends after all on the human resources at the disposal of any organization. A change is needed today in the co-operative banks which is built on confidence in human capital—the most important of all resources—in commitment, creativity and innovation brought about by proactive management, membership and employees. Strong corporate governance that takes its obligations seriously can truly be a source of strength to the management. The ability to capture knowledge and wisdom gives co-operative banks their competitive advantage. A prerequisite is that participants from all parts of a co-operative organization know and understand its purpose, core values and visions.

Measures Taken by Regulator Towards Corporate Governance

Regulators are external pressure points for good corporate governance. Mere compliance with regulatory requirements is not however an ideal situation in itself. In fact, mere compliance with regulatory pressures is a minimum requirement of good corporate governance and what are required are internal pressures, peer pressures and market pressures to reach higher than minimum standards prescribed by regulatory agencies. RBI's approach to regulation in recent times has some features that would enhance the need for and usefulness of good corporate governance in the co-operative sector. Reserve Bank of India has taken various steps furthering corporate governance in the Indian Banking System. These can broadly be classified into the following three categories:

(a) Transparency

(b) Off-site surveillance

(c) Prompt corrective action

(d) Investment ceiling

Transparency

The Transparency aspect has been Emphasized by expanding the coverage of information and timeliness of such information and analytical content. Importantly, deregulation and operational freedom must go hand in hand with operational transparency. In fact, the RBI Governor's April 2002 Monetary and Credit Policy announcements have made it clear that with the abolition of minimum lending rates for co-operative banks, it will be incumbent on these banks to make the interest rates charged by them transparent and known to all customers. Banks have therefore been asked to publish the minimum and maximum interest rates charged by them and display this information in every branch. Disclosure and transparency are thus key pillars of a corporate governance framework because they provide all the stakeholders with the information necessary to judge whether their interests are being taken care of. RBI see transparency and disclosure as an important adjunct to the supervisory process as they facilitate market discipline of banks.

Another area which requires focused attention is greater transparency in the balance sheets of co-operative banks. The commercial banks in India are now required to disclose accounting ratios relating to operating profit, return on assets, business per employee, NPAs, etc. as also maturity profile of loans, advances, investments, borrowings and deposits. The issue before us now is how to adapt similar disclosures suitably to be captured in the audit reports of co-operative banks. RBI had advised Registrars of Co-operative Societies of the state governments in 1996 that the balance sheet and profit & loss account should be prepared based on prudential norms introduced as a sequel to Financial Sector Reforms and that the statutory/departmental auditors of co-operative banks should look into the compliance with these norms. Auditors are therefore expected to be well-versed with all aspects of the new guidelines issued by RBI and ensure that the profit & loss account and balance sheet of co-operative banks are prepared in a transparent manner and reflect the true state of affairs. Auditors should also ensure that other necessary statutory provisions and appropriations out of profits are made as required in terms of the Co-operative Societies Act / Rules of the state concerned and the bye-laws of the respective institutions.

Off-site Surveillance Mechanism

The off-site surveillance mechanism is also active in monitoring the movement of assets, its impact on capital adequacy and overall efficiency and adequacy of managerial practices in banks. RBI also brings out the periodic data on "Peer Group Comparison" on critical ratios to maintain peer pressure for better performance and governance.

Prompt Corrective Action

Prompt corrective action has been adopted by RBI as a part of core principles for effective banking supervision. As against a single trigger point based on capita adequacy normally adopted by many countries, Reserve Bank in keeping with Indian conditions have set two more trigger points namely Non-Performing Assets (NPA) and Return on Assets (ROA) as proxies for asset quality and profitability. These trigger points will enable the intervention of regulator through a set of mandatory action to stem further deterioration in the health of banks showing signs of weakness.

Investment Ceiling

Investment Ceiling Banks were advised that only brokers registered with NSE or BSE or OTCEI should be utilized for acting as intermediary. If the deal is put through a broker, the role of the broker should be restricted to that of bringing the two parties to the transaction together. The settlement of the transaction, namely, both funds settlement and security settlement should be made directly between the counter parties. With a view to ensuring that a disproportionate volume of transactions is not routed through one or a few broker, a prudential ceiling of 5 per cent of the total transactions (both purchases and sales) has been prescribed for routing transactions through an individual broker. In case any bank is required to exceed the prudential ceiling of 5 per cent for any broker, the bank is required to inform the Board indicating the reasons therefore post-facto. Banks have also been advised to have proper internal control measures for monitoring the transactions in Government securities.

Conlusion

In the years to come, the Indian financial system will grow not only in size but also in complexity as the forces of competition gain further momentum and financial markets acquire greater depth. I can assure you that the policy environment will remain supportive of healthy growth and development with accent on more operational flexibility as well as greater prudential regulation and supervision. The real success of our financial sector reforms will however depend primarily on the organizational effectiveness of the banks, including cooperative banks, for which initiatives will have to come from the banks itself. It is for the co-operative banks itself to build on the synergy inherent in the cooperative structure and stand up for their unique qualities. With elements of good corporate governance, sound investment policy, appropriate internal control systems, better credit risk management, focus on newly-emerging business areas like micro finance, commitment to better customer service, adequate automation and proactive policies on house-keeping issues, co-operative banks will definitely be able to grapple with these challenges and convert them into opportunities.

References

1. Abiman Das (1999), “Profitability of Public Sector Banks” A Decomposition Model, July, 55-81.
2. Angadis, V.B. and Devaraj, V.J. (1983) “Productivity and Profitability of Banks in India”, *Economic and Political Weekly,* November, Vol.18(26): 48.
3. Amitab Tiwari (1981), “Banking for Development in India”, *Southern Economist*, April, Vol. 15 (8): 12-13.
4. Patel, A. R. (1995), “Rural Banking: Service Area Policy Shift Needed”, *Kisan World*, August 1, Vol. 34(4)17.
5. Ashok K. Nag and Abiman Das (2002), “Credit Growth and Response to Capital Requirements”, *Economic and Political Weakly*, August Vol. XXXVII; (32) 2460-2467.
6. Bhairav. H. Desai (2002), “Concept of Break Even Analysis and Bank Profitability—A Case Study”, *The Indian Journal of Commerce*, Vol. 53, No.182. pp. 53-59.

7. Charan D. Wadhwa (1980), *Rural Bank for Rural Development,* Macmillan and Company Delhi.
8. http://www.rbi.in/scripts/BS-view Bulletin7135.
9. http://www.rbi.in/scripts/BS-view Bulletin6696.
10. http://www.rbi.org.in/scripts/BS-view Bulletin7211.

2

Corporate Governance in India
Lessons and Actions

Dr. Ashok Kumar Panigrahi

ABSTRACT

The Corporate Governance, has never, since the Satyam Episode, become such a buzzword for the Indian corporate world. The Satyam scandal certainly raises serious questions about corporate governance. Ramalinga Raju's disclosures regarding forging accounts of Satyam have come as a deep shock and disappointment for corporate India, which feels the development, will have a major impact on investors, clients and employees, going ahead. Industry players also aware that there is a need to immediately examine the loopholes in regulation, accounting, audit and governance that allowed such lapses to occur and address them with urgency as this has shaken the confidence of investors—both domestic and global—the repercussions of which could be felt over the medium-term. The issue is all the more grave since this has happened to an Indian MNC, which has received, ironically, accolades for good corporate governance. No doubt this has put a question mark on the entire corporate governance system in India. In this paper an attempt is made to highlight the lessons learnt by corporate India from Satyam scandal and actions taken so far to reform the Indian corporate governance system.

Learning's from Satyam Scandal

The apex body of chartered accountants, Institute of Chartered Accountants of India believes that Satyam scam is the best things that could happen, as in the near future, it would help to improve the level of corporate governance in the country, reports economic times.

Amarjit Chopra, President, ICAI said, "Satyam is a study in itself and a matter of research also. I think in periods to come you will find that it will help to improve the levels of corporate governance in the country. Probably, Satyam is the best things that could happen because it shall now prevent frauds in future."

Telling about the lessons learnt from Satyam scam, Chopra said that the multi-crore Satyam scam is a case study before the fraternity, which was primarily more a scandal of corporate governance. "It was the failure of audit committee chairman to raise the issue of funds to the tune of Rs 2,000 crore lying in Satyam's current account, otherwise the scam could have surfaced much earlier. In the wake of this magnitude of the scam we have urged the government to fix obligation of independent directors and what kind of role they can play in a firm."

The Satyam scandal certainly raises serious questions about corporate governance. These questions will not stop at Satyam. Many more companies will get into a scrutiny like that. The collapse of Lehman Brothers, one of the world's most reputed global financial services firms, dealt a rude blow to the world last year. But, despite the shock, Indians could afford to take a clinical look at it from afar. In fact, even the 2001 Enron scandal in the US, which involved irregular accounting procedures, was perhaps nothing more than news on the foreign page. But, with the Satyam's fabricated balance sheets fiasco hitting much closer to home, it would seem Indians have front-row seats this time. And today, one cannot help but question the role of corporate governance.

According to Rekha Sethi, director general, All India Management Association (AIMA), "The whole idea behind corporate governance is ensuring the accountability of certain individuals in an organization through mechanisms that try to reduce or eliminate unfair practices within the corporate system." So, corporate governance is all about transparency.

The Satyam episode has brought out the failure of the present corporate governance structure. The present corporate governance structure hinges on the independent directors, who are supposed to bring objectivity to the oversight function of the board and improve its effectiveness. Stakeholders place high expectation on them. But is the expectation misplaced? Perhaps, yes.

An individual independent director cannot play an effective role in isolation. Even if a particular independent director is highly committed, he/she can only 'watch' wrong doing and at best initiate a discussion, but alone he/she cannot stop a decision even if it is detrimental to the interest of shareholders or other stakeholders. Neither can he/she blow the whistle outside the board room (e.g. to regulators) because board proceedings are considered confidential.

The only way independent directors can stop wrong decisions is by acting collectively. Even then they can seldom be expected to stop 'management fraud' since turning independent directors into policemen in the board room will have excessive detrimental effects on the independence of directors, the freedom of enterprise of the managers and the costs of governance. In discharging its responsibility of ensuring adequate and effective internal control the board must depend on other institutions of corporate governance such as internal audit, external audit, and legal counsel. Therefore, the effectiveness of independent directors depends significantly on the independence and effectiveness of those institutions. Independent directors may not be in a position to stop management fraud perpetrated at the highest level, but with high level of commitment and due diligence they should be able to identify signals that indicate that everything is not hunky dory.

There are quite a few lessons to be learnt from the Satyam fiasco. First, there has to be stringent enforcement of the existing regulation and legislative rules across different ownership structures. Second, directors who guide the board should meet independent of the management in times of crisis. And third, since board members may be constrained by certain information, which can lead to less informed decisions, they should insist on additional data and also try to verify the information provided for a decision-making process.

India vowed to strengthen laws to prevent corporate fraud after Satyam Scam, the country's fourth-largest software company, shocked investors by revealing profits had been falsely inflated for years. "The government will take all necessary action to ensure these types of scandals do not take place again. Whatever steps could be taken will be taken," Corporate Affairs Minister Prem Chand Gupta told on Satyam scandal. The scandal has cast a cloud over foreign investment in Asia's third-largest economy and over its once-booming outsourcing sector, which posted stunning sales growth for years and lavished investors with handsome returns. It may also increase investor nervousness about weak corporate governance and oversight in emerging markets, which are still reeling from the global financial crisis. Meanwhile, the Associated Chambers of Commerce and Industry of India has suggested setting up of a special committee to investigate the entire issue so that culprits are identified and brought to book. According to the Chamber, the government should hasten process of investigating the matter so that the confidence of investors in Indian corporate world is retained and not shaken at any cost.

The issue is all the more grave since this has happened to an Indian MNC, which has received, ironically, accolades for good corporate governance. "The news certainly came as a surprise," said Ranjit Shahani, vice-chairman and MD of Novartis India Limited. "While we have all the right mechanisms in place to prevent such happenings, the regulatory authorities need to step in to check why these mechanisms failed. Going forward, one can expect to see increased focus on good corporate governance and the role independent directors should play." There will be heightened scrutiny as this is the first large Indian multinational company to walk this path.

The Satyam controversy could certainly have a direct impact on the IT sector most of which is cash-rich, but more than that it is likely to push corporate India to look within and ensure better governance.

In the short term, investors will start looking deeper into all companies they want to invest in, and rightly so. Once they realize that things are not all that bad and that most companies are decent and managements honest, they will regain their faith.

Indian CG System after Satyam Scam

Corporate India will never be the same again. What transpired in Satyam computers in January culminating into the historic confession letter of former chairman B. Ramalinga Raju, admitting a fraud of Rs. 78 billion has caused the regulators and the investors everywhere to re-examine the corporate governance standards. The multi billion dollar scam is unprecedented and idiosyncratic for more than one reason. The fact that company which was audited by one of the most prestigious audit firms and adopted most advanced accounting and transparent IFRS accounting systems much ahead of time can penetrate such a colossal and a global fraud is clearly eye opening for corporate counsel worldwide. It was triggered with Satyam's bid to acquire Maytas companies for US$1.6 billion.[1]This revealed the self aggrandizing policies of the promoters, which caused severe investor backlash.

While there are adequate levels of checks and balances in the system to prevent frauds, it is the slack attitude of each institution responsible for upholding corporate governance that made such a fraud possible. Unless heavy fines and strict liabilities are provided for, if not in the statute then in the internal code of conduct, each of these institutions, namely the internal audit committee, the independent directors and the external auditors could continue to remain "rubber stamps" approbating all management actions.[2]

The Satyam scandal has reiterated the importance of checks on related party transactions. Stringent checks and balances on these ought to be incorporated into the Indian corporate and securities laws to prevent transactions like Maytas in future. Pending statutory incorporation, companies can incorporate adequate checks and balances in their code of conduct as a measure of ensuring good corporate governance. It is natural to expect an enhanced level of security of the financial and governance aspects of Indian companies, and to a lesser extent, any Asian-based companies. The role of corporate counsel will assume added pressures, with a higher emphasis on preventing frauds.

In the area of securities regulation, SEBI has made numerous changes in recent years including: revising and strengthening Clause 49 in relation to independent directors and audit committees; revising Clause 41 of the Listing Agreement on interim and annual financial results; and amending other listing rules to protect the interests of minority shareholders, for example in mergers and acquisitions. SEBI brought out new rules in February 2009 requiring greater disclosure by promoters (i.e., controlling shareholders) of their shareholdings and any pledging of shares to third parties. And in November 2009 it announced, it would be making some further changes to the Listing Agreement, including requiring listed companies to produce half yearly balance sheets. More recently, in December 2009, the Ministry of Corporate Affairs (MCA) published a new set of "Corporate Governance Voluntary Guidelines 2009", designed to encourage companies to adopt better practices in the running of boards and board committees, the appointment and rotation of external auditors, and creating a whistle blowing mechanism.[3]

In the current corporate governance practices it is required to focus on particular corporate governance mechanisms. There are two types of mechanism that resolve the conflicts among different corporate claim-holders, especially, the conflicts between owners and managers, and those between controlling shareholders and minority shareholders. The first type consists of various internal variables, e.g. (1) the ownership structure, (2) board of directors, (3) executive compensation and (4) financial disclosure.[4]

The second includes external mechanism with variables, e.g. (1) effective takeover market, (2) legal infrastructure and (3) product market competition. 'Good corporate governance practices are a *sine qua non* for sustainable business that aims at generating long term value to all its shareholders and other stakeholders'.[5]

A more comprehensive review of corporate governance regulation and practices is required in India. While the new "Voluntary Guidelines 2009" provide helpful and detailed guidance to companies interested in developing a more effective board of directors yet lot of issues remain unattained and unanswered. Nor will the new Companies Bill resolve these challenges.

Independent Directors

Nomination committee can be advisably established comprising solely of independent directors or a majority of independent directors empowered to appoint the board and evaluate its performance. Although evaluation of performance is not yet mandatory under the extent of corporate governance regime yet it might yield a better result and in further coarse of time it should be made compulsory.

There should be a fixed tenure beyond which an independent director should not be associated with a company. An aggregate limit of nine years has been prescribed under clause 49 VII (ii) of the equity listing agreement, but such a requirement is not mandatory.[6]

Regarding the remuneration of the independent directors the pecuniary payouts are usually incommensurate with the onerous role they perform. Adequate remuneration may ensure that the directors discharge their duty with care and diligence rather than just playing an ornamental role in the organization. Another step that might ensure a better working is that the independent directors should meet separately without any member in the management to discuss the affairs of the company. This would help them to make decisions on matters without being euphemistically 'guided' by the management.[7]

Limit on Number of Directorships

In case an individual is a managing or whole-time director in a listed company, the number of companies at which such an individual can serve as non-executive director, be restricted to 10, and the number of listed companies at which such an individual can serve as a non-executive director, be restricted to 2. The maximum number of listed companies in which an individual can serve as a director is to be restricted to 7.[8]

Separation of roles of Chairman and CEO

There should be a clear demarcation of the roles and responsibilities of the Chairman of the Board and that of the Managing Director/CEO. The Roles of Chairman and CEO should be separated to promote balance of power. A "comply or explain" approach should be adopted.[9]

Auditors

Compulsory rotation of auditors Though there are views that periodic rotation of the audit firm may be enough to break the collusive links between the company and the auditors. The alternatives to rotation are joint audit, rotating of managing partners, harsh penalties for collusion and regulation will make it difficult for the companies to sack the auditors who insist on qualifying fudged accounts. SEBI released on September 14, 2009 on proposed changes to the Listing Agreement, one of the reforms suggested was the rotation of either audit firms or audit partners as a way to enhance their independence from clients.[10]

SEBI felt that the independence of auditors should be reviewed because, as it said in its discussion paper: "The quality of financials reported by companies and the true and fair view of the financial statements submitted by listed entities to the stock exchanges have, of late, come into sharp focus."[11]

Moreover, in India, there is no supervisory structure like the PCAOB in US which is an independent body which supervises the audit of public firms.... a similar structure should be mandated for Indian audits.[12]

Secretarial Audit

Secretarial Audit should be made mandatory in respect of listed companies and certain other companies. The report on the audit of secretarial records shall be submitted by the secretarial auditor to the Corporate Compliance Committee of the Board of Directors of the company. The Secretarial Audit Report should form part of the Board's Report.

Risk Management

Companies need to frame a strong risk management framework to systematically manage and regularly review the risk profile at a strategic, operational and functional level. Whistle blowers policy which is ingrained in the model code of conduct of a few corporations in India should be made mandatory for all the listed companies to encourage transparency.[13]

Listed companies must have a nominating/corporate governance committee composed entirely of independent board members. The committee must have a written charter that addresses its purpose and responsibilities, which include *(i)* identifying qualified individuals to become board member; *(ii)* selecting, or recommending that the board select, the director nominees for the next annual meeting of shareholders; *(iii)* developing and recommending to the board a set of corporate governance principles applicable to the company; *(iv)* overseeing the evaluation of the board and management; and *(v)* conducting an annual performance evaluation of the committee.[14]

Corporate Compliance Committee to be Made Mandatory

The constitution of Corporate Compliance Committee should be made mandatory in respect of all public limited companies having a paid-up capital of Rs.5 crores or more.[15]

Directors' Responsibility Statement to Include Statement on Compliances

Directors' Responsibility Statement should include a statement that proper systems are in place to ensure compliance of all laws applicable to the company.

Constitution of Investor Relations Cell

Constitution of Investor Relations Cell should be made mandatory for Listed Companies. The Investor Relations meet after declaration of financial results should be compulsorily webcast in case of companies having a market capitalization of Rs.1000 Crores or more.[16]

The Ministry of Corporate Affairs (MCA) based on Satyam fraud investigation has worked out new parameters for scrutiny of companies. In instructions to the Registrar of Companies (RoC), MCA has pointed to 'cash at bank' as a vital parameter for scrutiny.[17]

Till now, the auditor's certificate was sufficient. After the Satyam episode, it has been decided that the RoC should not only look at the balance sheet but also check the veracity of the certificates. This could be done either internally or in coordination with other regulators. The RoC will now not only verify cash at bank but also cross-check. In the case of Satyam, which had shown Rs. 3,800 crore as cash at bank, the auditors had relied on a bank statement provided by the company. The auditors are required to confirm from the bank to verify the amount. It is important to check this parameter, as it indicates the financial health of the company, based on which company's shareholders; analysts and other outsiders make an assessment.

Various counter arguments are made in India against introducing stronger rules on related-party transactions. One is that allowing shareholders to vote on such transactions would interfere with the smooth operation of companies. Another is that since many promoters (i.e., controlling shareholders) have more than 50 per cent of the voting rights in the company, the result of any vote would be a foregone conclusion. These objections miss the point: as rules in other markets show, related-party regulation does not require every single transaction to be voted on—only the largest and most material. Moreover, the second objection is not relevant, since connected shareholders would not be permitted to vote in a meeting of independent shareholders it is not just the voting power that is sought to be a check on related party transactions, when such a transactions require shareholder approval, then the board has to justify it to the shareholders. This is the bigger check. Even though they may have the required voting strength, other shareholders can still ask questions and the board will have to justify the deal. This will force the board not to enter into transactions that will bring it unwanted publicity.

SEBI only recently published regulations in the "Issue of Capital and Disclosure Requirements, 2009," which replaced the "Disclosure and Investor Protection Guidelines, 2000." Whereas the earlier regulations made scant reference to related-party transactions (other than the fact that promoters/controlling shareholders should disclose them in their financial reports), the new regulations do devote a paragraph on how related-party transactions should be disclosed according to Accounting Standard.[18]

"If more than 50 per cent of business transactions by a company are with related parties, then the balance sheet should be scrutinized and adequate explanations should be sought from its officers. Under this, if a company is using more than half its funds in activities other than the stated objective in the Memorandum of Association (MoU) given to the registrar of companies, the balance sheet will be examined. These purposes could be loans to subsidiary companies, other companies, and investments in mutual funds or stock market, real estate or in foreign exchange transactions when the company does not have much business with foreign exchange exposure, etc.[19]

A comprehensive regulation of related-party transactions, including giving independent shareholders the powers to approve large transactions above a certain limit and enhancing disclosure requirements on other material transactions. Such regulation could be provided for in both the Listing Agreement and new SEBI regulations or guidelines. An independent financial advisor and an independent board committee should be appointed to determine whether material transactions are fair and reasonable to all shareholders. Independent directors are required to exercise their duties more diligently and protect the interests of minority shareholders, especially in cases where the majority shareholder is also the manager of the company.[20]

Some degree of legal liability could be considered for directors in cases such as Satyam. Listed companies with numerous related transactions should set up a related-party transaction committee of their board. This would scrutinize such transactions, recommend to the board if shareholder approval should be sought, advise on disclosure and judge the fairness of transactions.

Corporate Disclosure

The scope, depth, timeliness, consistency and formatting of corporate financial disclosure in India could be greatly improved. Certain reforms are needed to improve the quality and timeliness of corporate disclosure of most listed companies in India. Such reforms would provide investors with more useful information on which to make investment decisions and would strengthen the reputation of the Indian capital market.[21]

All companies should, in effect, be required to produce audited annual results within three months of the year end and their full annual report within four, or at most five, months of the year end. The format of quarterly P&L statements is to be reviewed to require additional details regarding revenues. Listed companies are to be encouraged to provide both cash flow statements and balance sheets with their quarterly reports.

Corp Filing and EDIFAR (Electronic Data Information Filing and Retrieval System) should be merged into one database, with the structure following the organization of EDIFAR, but with further thought being given as to how information could be even more easily accessible.

On November 9, 2009, the SEBI Board announced that it would amend the Listing Agreement in relation to three of these issues, namely:

- Allowing the voluntary adoption of IFRS by listed entities with subsidiaries;
- Requiring half yearly disclosure of balance sheets (which must provide audited figures, or non-audited figures with limited review); and
- Approving some of the new deadlines recommended by SCODA for the submission of financial results. (Namely, a more flexible requirement for the disclosure of quarterly results—45 days after the period end rather than the current 30 days—but a tighter deadline for the disclosure of audited annual results by companies that opt to produce "stand-alone" (i.e.,unconsolidated) annual results instead of an unaudited fourth quarter report—reduced from 90 days to 60 days.)[22]

It is not clear, however, when these listing rule changes will take effect. Moreover, the changes to the disclosure deadlines still fail to address the problem of when a company should publish its audited annual results if it chooses to produce an unaudited fourth quarter report.[23]

Preferential Warrants

The scope for the misuse and abuse of warrants in India is considerable. Regulation of their issuance to promoters needs to be tightened. The issuance of preferential shares, warrants or other securities to promoters and other connected persons must be prohibited (as in other markets), except under the limited circumstances envisaged in markets such as Hong Kong (i.e., where the securities are part of a pro-rata entitlement made available to all shareholders on an equal basis, or as part of a shareholder-approved stock option scheme).[24]

Companies are required to seek shareholder approval at their annual general meetings for the issuance, over the subsequent 12 months, of any new shares at a discount to a limited group of (non-controlling) shareholders. Strict rules should govern the size and discount of such offerings. Listed companies should review the way they use warrants and limit their application to forming part of a wider issue of debt or equity securities (i.e., where warrants act as sweeteners for investors).

Conclusion

The Satyam incident, though unfortunate, exposed some big loopholes in the system. Just as the United States needed the Enron scandal to clean up its act, perhaps India needed the Satyam fiasco to introduce sweeping changes in its own financial reporting system. It cannot be denied that the Satyam episode was a stark failure of the code of Corporate Governance in India. Corporate governance refers to an economic, legal and institutional environment that allows companies diversify, grow, restructure and exit, and do everything necessary to maximize long term shareholder value. It is not something which can be enforced by mere legislation; it is a way of life and has to imbibe itself into the very business culture the company operates in. Ultimately, following practices of good governance leads to all round benefits for all the parties concerned. The company's reputation is boosted, the shareholders and creditors are empowered due to the transparency Corporate Governance brings in, the employees enjoy the improved systems of management and the community at large enjoys the fruits of better economic growth in a responsible way. The loyalty of a typical Indian investor is far greater than his counterparts in the USA or Britain.[25]

But, our companies must not make the mistake of taking such loyalty as a given. To nurture and strengthen this loyalty, our companies need to give a clear-cut signal that the words "your company" have real meaning. That requires well functioning boards, greater disclosure, better management practices, and a more open, interactive and dynamic corporate governance environment. Quite simply, shareholders' and creditors' support are vital for the survival, growth and competitiveness of India's companies. Such support requires us to tone up our act today.

References

1. Berger A. N. and Bonaccorsidi Patti E (2006), "Capital Structure and Firm Performance: A New Approach to Testing Agency and An Application to the Banking Industry", *Journal of Banking and Finance*, Vol.30, No.4, pp.1065-1102.
2. Basel Committee on Banking Supervision (BCBS) (1999), "Enhancing Corporate Governance for Banking Organizations", Bank for International Settlements, Switzerland. King and Levine (1993a and b).
3. Bajaj, R., Chairman (1997), *Draft Code on Corporate Governance,* Confederation of Indian Industry.
4. Bhatia D.K. (2000), 'Corporate Governance', in Corporate Sector Research Conference Volume, held at Navi Mumbai during 12th May, 2000, pp. A35-A57.
5. Bhattacharya Ashis K (1996), 'Corporate Governance', The Chartered Accountant, November, pp. 14-23.
6. Berger A.N., Hunter W. C. and Timme S. G. (1993), "The Efficiency of Financial Institutions: A Review and Preview of Research Past, Present and Future", *Journal of Banking and finance,* Vol.17, pp.221-249.
7. Becht M, Bolton P. and Roell A. A. (2003), "Corporate Governance and Control", in Costantinides G, Harris M and Stulz R (Eds), *Handbook of the Economics of Finance*, Amsterdam, North Holland.
8. Cadbury Committee (1992), Report of the Committee on the Financial Aspects of Corporate Governance, Gee London.
9. Corporate Governance–International Journal for Enhancing Board Performance Vol.1, 2003.
10. Corporate Governance: A Framework for Implementation–Overview (1999, World Bank)
11. Davies Adrian., A Strategic Approach To Corporate Governance, Gower, Gower House, Croft Road, England.
12. Damiani M (2006), Impresa Corporate Governance, Roma, Carocci.
13. Elson, C.M and C.J. Gyves (2002); *The Enron Failure and Corporate Governance Reforms*.

14. Elankumaran S (2006), "Corporate Codes of Conduct in India: A Survey", *Journal of Human Values,* Vol. 12, pp.65.

15. Freeman R.B.(1990), "Corporate Governance: A Stakeholder Interpretation", *Journal of Behavioral Economics,* Vol.19, No. 4, pp.337-360.

16. Gopal K. (1998),"Emerging Trends in Corporate Governance", *The Management Accountant, June,* pp. 420-570.

17. Gordon, E and Natarajan, K. Banking Theory, Law and Practices, Himalaya Publishing House.

18. Gugler K (2001), *Corporate Governance and Economic Performance,* Oxford University Press, Oxford.

19. Jiraporn P., Kim Y.S., Davidson W.N. and Singh M. (2006), "Corporate Governance, Shareholder Rights and Firm Diversification: An Empirical Analysis", *Journal of Banking and Finance,* Vol.30, No.3, pp.947-963.

20. John, Kose and Senbet, W. Lemma (1998); Corporate Governance and Board Effectiveness; *Journal of Banking and Finance,* pp. 371-403.

21. Kaplan,S.N (1997), *Corporate Governance and Corporate Performance,* Oxford University Press, New York.

22. Kamesam Vepa (2006), "Corporate Best Practices: Recommendations for Directors", IRDA Journal (March), pp. 26-29.

23. Kondap, N.M.,Corporate Governance–Corporate Social Responsibility; Indian Case Study.

24. Kumar Mangalam Birla Committee on Corporate Governance (2000).

Notes

1. http://economictimes. indiatimes.com/infotech/software/Post-satyam-Adding-teeth-to-Corporate-Governance/articleshow/5334750.cms.

2. Satyam fraud can be the greatest threat to corporate reputation of India, by Rahul, available at, http:www.indiaedunews.net/pressreleases/Users/Satyam_fraud_can_be_the_greatest-threat_to_the_corporate_repuation_of_India-1.asp,last visited on 16.3.10.

3. www.mca.gov.in

4. Internal Control-Integrated Framework: executive summary, available at http://www.tubitak.gov.tr/tubitak_content_files//

icdenetim/ekutuphane/COSOInternalControlStandards.doc, last visited on 11.3.10.

5. Corporate Governance Voluntary guidelines 2009: A study, available at http://www.nehasinghi.com/archives/corporate-governance-voluntary-guidelines-2009-a-study, last visited on 25.3.10.
6. The good thing about the Satyam fiasco, http://www.dare.co.in/blog-entries/in-the-news/the-good-thing-about-the-satyam-fiasco.htm.
7. Dr. C.S. Bansal, *Corporate Governance Law Practice & Practice* (Taxmann Allied Services P.Ltd. 2005 ed.), p.116.
8. http://www.taxguru.in/company-law/icsi-submits-recommendations-to-shri-salman-khurshid-to-strengthen-corporate-governance-framework.html.
9. *Ibid*
10. http://www.sebi.gov.in/Index. jsp? content Disp= Committee.
11. Discussion paper on proposals relating to amendments to the Listing Agreement, available at http://www.sebi.gov.in/commreport/amendproposal.pdf, last visited on 23.3.10.
12. The Great Deception, available at http://www.asialaw.com/Article/2097602/Channel/16709/The-great-deception.html, last visited on 15.3.10.
13. http://meetjohndoe.sulekha.com/blog/post/2009/07/corporate-governance-satyam-and-beyond.htm, last visited on 20.3.10
14. Satyam's principal corporate governance practices available on www.caclubindia.com/.../satyam-s-principal-corporate-governance-practices-21744.asp?...Last visited on 15.3.10.
15. http://www.riskadvisory.net/uploads/India%20satyam20 (3).pdf.
16. Press release, December 2009, available at http://www.icsi.edu/Webmodules/LinksofWeeks/Press%20Release_mca.doc, last visited on 22.3.10.
17. MCA announced new parameters for scrutiny of companies, cash at bank vital parameter for scrutiny, available at, http://www.taxguru.in/company-law/mca-announced-new-parameters-for-scrutiny-of-companies-cash-at-bank-vital-parameter-for-scrutiny.html#ixzz0jlOT5v71, last visited on 12.3.10.
18. www.sebi.gov.in
19. http://www.business-standard.com/india/news/post-satyam-mca-lays-new-scrutiny-rules/379715/

20. The Great Deception, available at http://www.asialaw.com/Article/2097602/Channel/16709/The-great-deception.html, last visited on 15.3.10.
21. http://docs.google.com/viewer?a=v&q=cache: hUFe 2LTGNew: www.dsklegal.com/pdf_new/Volume-V-VI-DSK%2520Legal%2520Knowledge%2520Update%2520Update%2520%2520%SEBI. pdf+ corporate+disclosure+and+investor+protection+ub+india&hl+eb&in&pid=bl&srcid=ADGEEShB, last visited on 20.3.10.
22. http://www.sebi.gov.in/Index. jsp? content Disp=Committee.
23. http://www.acga-asia.org/public/files/ACGA_India_White_Paper_Final_Jan19_2010.pdf.
24. *Ibid.*
25. Desirable Corporate Governance: A Code, available at www.ciionline.org , last visited on 17.3.10.

3

Corporate Governance in Banks

Ms. Vimla Virparia

ABSTRACT

The concept of corporate governance, which emerged as a response to corporate failures and widespread dissatisfaction with the way many corporates function, has become one of the wide and deep discussions across the globe recently. It primarily hinges on complete transparency, integrity and accountability of the management. There is also an increasingly greater focus on investor protection and public interest. Corporate governance is concerned with the values, vision and visibility. It is about the value orientation of the organisation, ethical norms for its performance, the direction of development and social accomplishment of the organisation and the visibility of its performance and practices. This article highlights the role and importance of corporate governance in banking sectors.

Genesis of Corporate Governance

It will certainly not be out of place here to recount how issues relating to corporate governance and corporate control have come to the fore the world over in the recent past. The seeds of modern corporate governance were probably sown by the Watergate scandal in the USA. Such spectacular corporate failures arose primarily out of poorly managed business practices.

In May 1991, the London Stock Exchange set up a Committee under the chairmanship of Sir Arian Cadbury to help raise the standards of corporate governance and the level of confidence in financial reporting and auditing by setting out clearly what it sees as the respective responsibilities of those involved and what it believes is expected of them. Governance needed to achieve a balance between the essential powers of the Board of Directors and their proper accountability.

Board of Directors should meet regularly, retain full and effective control over the company and monitor the executive management. There should be a clearly accepted division of responsibilities.

The Cadbury Report generated a lot of interest in India. The issue of corporate governance was studied in depth and dealt with by the Confederation of Indian Industries (CII), Associated Chamber of Commerce and Industry (ASSOCHAM) and Securities and Exchange Board of India (SEBI).

Introduction

Corporate Governance is now an issue and important factor that can be used as tool to maximize wealth of shareholders of a corporate. Corporate Governance aims ar the following:

- Vision
- Values
- Visibility

Vision means direction towards which the corporate is moving, *value* means the value orientation of the corporate, *visibility* means transparency in terms of its performance and practices.

Definition

Corporate governance is the set of processes, customs, policies, laws, and institutions affecting the way a corporation (or company) is directed, administered or controlled. Corporate governance also includes the relationships among the many stakeholders involved and the goals for which the corporation is governed

Corporate governance is a multi-faceted subject. An important theme of corporate governance is to ensure the accountability of certain individuals in an organization through mechanisms that try to reduce or eliminate the principal-agent problem.

Why Corporate Governance in Bank?

Generally banks occupy a delicate position in the economic equation of any country such that its performance invariably affects the economy of the country. Poor corporate governance may contribute to bank failures, which can pose significant public costs and consequences due to their potential impact on any applicable deposit insurance systems and the possibility of broader macroeconomic implications such as contagion risk and impact on payment systems. In addition, poor corporate governance can lead markets to lose confidence in the ability of a bank to properly manage its assets and liabilities, including deposits which could turn trigger a bank run or liquidity crisis.

Objective

- Establishing strategic objectives and a set of corporate values that are communicated throughout the banking organisation;
- Setting and enforcing clear lines of responsibility and accountability throughout the organisation;
- Ensuring that board members are qualified for their positions, have a clear understanding of their role in corporate governance and are not subject to undue influence from management or outside concerns;

- Ensuring that there is appropriate oversight by senior management;
- Effectively utilising the work conducted by internal and external auditors, in recognition of the important control function they provide;
- Ensuring that compensation approaches are consistent with the bank's ethical values, objectives, strategy and control environment;
- Conducting corporate governance in a transparent manner.

Corporate Governance in Bank

In the case of traditional manufacturing corporations, the issue has been that of safeguarding and maximizing the shareholders' value. In the case of banking, the risk involved for depositors and the possibility of contagion assumes greater importance than that of consumers of manufactured products. Further, the involvement of government is discernibly higher in banks due to importance of stability of financial system and the larger interests of the public. Since the market control is not sufficient to ensure proper governance in banks, the government does see reason in regulating and controlling the nature of activities, the structure of bonds, the ownership pattern, capital adequacy norms, liquidity ratios, etc.

Role of the Government and the Regulator

Regulators are external pressure points for good corporate governance. RBI's approach to regulation in recent times has some features that would enhance the need for and usefulness of good corporate governance in the co-operative sector. The transparency aspect has been emphasized by expanding the coverage of information and timeliness of such information and analytical content. The RBI has made it clear that with the abolition of minimum lending rates for co-operative banks, it will be incumbent on these banks to make the interest rates, charged by them, transparent and known to all customers. Banks have therefore been asked to publish the minimum and maximum interest rates charged by them and display this information in every branch. Disclosure and transparency are thus key pillars of a corporate governance framework because they provide all the stakeholders with the information necessary to judge whether their interests are being taken care of.

Another area which requires focused attention is greater transparency in the balance sheets of co-operative banks. The commercial banks in India are now required to disclose accounting ratios relating to operating profit, return on assets, business per employee, NPAs, etc. as also maturity profile of loans, advances, investments, borrowings and deposits.

Auditors are therefore expected to be well-versed with all aspects of the new guidelines issued by RBI and ensure that the profit and loss account and balance sheet of cooperative banks are prepared in a transparent manner and reflect the true state of affairs. Auditors should also ensure that other necessary statutory provisions and appropriations out of profits are made as required in the terms of Co-operative Societies Act/Rules of the state concerned and the bye-laws of the respective institutions.

Role of Board of Directors and their Committees

At the initiative of the RBI, a consultative group, aimed at strengthening corporate governance in banks, headed by Dr. Ashok Ganguli was set up to review the supervisory role of Board of banks. The recommendations include the role and responsibility of independent non-executive directors, qualification and other eligibility criteria for appointment of non-executive directors, training of the directors and keeping them update with the latest developments. Some of the important recommendations on the constitution of the Board are:

- Participate in the meetings of the board regularly and ensure that their participation is effective and contributory.

- They must study the reports submitted to them by the management team and enquire about follow up reports on definite time schedule. They should be actively involved in the formulation of general policies.
- They should be familiar with the road objectives of the bank and the policies laid down by the govt. and the changes in the various laws and legislations time to time.
- They should also ensure confidentiality of the banks agendas papers, notes and minutes of the meetings.
- They should not interfere in the day to day functioning of the bank.
- They should be loyal to the bank and must remember that they should not reveal any information relating to any constituent of the bank to anyone.
- They should not sponsor any proposal relating to loans, investments, buildings or sites for banks premises, enlistment or empanelment of contractors, architects, auditors, doctors etc.
- They should do only those things that are legal and acceptable.
- They should promote good and fair banking practices by setting proper benchmarks in dealing with customers.

Measures Taken by Banks towards Implementation of Best Practices

Prudential Norms in terms of income recognition, asset classification, and capital adequacy have been well assimilated by the Indian banking system. In keeping with the international best practice, starting 31st March 2004, banks have adopted 90 days norm for classification of NPAs. Also, norms governing provisioning requirements in respect of doubtful assets have been made more stringent in a phased manner. Beginning 2005, banks will be required to set aside capital charge for market risk on their trading portfolio of government investments, which was earlier virtually exempt from market risk requirement.

Capital Adequacy: All the Indian banks, barring one, today are well above the stipulated benchmark of 9 per cent and remain in a state of preparedness to achieve the best standards of CRAR as soon as the new Basel 2 norms are made operational. In fact, as of 31st March 2004, banking system as a whole had a CRAR close to 13 per cent.

On the Income Recognition Front, there is complete uniformity now in the banking industry and the system therefore ensures responsibility and accountability on the part of the management in proper accounting of income as well as loan impairment.

ALM and Risk Management Practices At the initiative of the regulators, banks were quickly required to address the need for Asset Liability Management followed by risk management practices. Both these are critical areas for an effective oversight by the Board and the senior management which are implemented by the Indian banking system on a tight time frame and the implementation review by RBI. These steps have enabled banks to understand, measure and anticipate the impact of the interest rate risk and liquidity risk, which in deregulated environment is gaining importance.

Measures Taken by Regulator towards Corporate Governance

Reserve Bank of India has taken various steps furthering corporate governance in the Indian Banking System. These can broadly be classified into the following three categories:

(a) Transparency

(b) Off-site surveillance

(c) Prompt corrective action

Transparency and disclosure standards are also important constituents of a sound corporate governance mechanism. Transparency and accounting standards in India have been enhanced to align with international best practices. However, there are many gaps in the disclosures in India vis-à-vis the international standards, particularly in the area of risk management strategies and risk parameters, risk concentrations, performance measures, component of capital structure, etc. Hence, the disclosure standards need to be further broad-based in consonance with improvements in the capability of market players to analyze the information objectively.

The off-site surveillance mechanism is also active in monitoring the movement of assets, its impact on capital adequacy and overall efficiency and adequacy of managerial practices in banks. RBI also brings out the periodic data on "Peer Group Comparison" on critical ratios to maintain peer pressure for better performance and governance.

Prompt corrective action has been adopted by RBI as a part of core principles for effective banking supervision. As against a single trigger point based on capita adequacy normally adopted by many countries, Reserve Bank of India in keeping with Indian conditions have set two more trigger points namely Non-Performing Assets (NPA) and Return on Assets (ROA) as proxies for asset quality and profitability. These trigger points will enable the intervention of regulator through a set of mandatory action to stem further deterioration in the health of banks showing signs of weakness.

Challenges

There are three major challenges facing governance ratings in India:

- Firstly there does not seem to be a clear objective in relation to the capital markets.
- The second challenge is that there is insufficient accumulated knowledge on corporate governance and a great amount of fluidity in the theory at present.
- The third challenge is to assign weightings to the companies in the context of global markets. The rating agencies need to reflect on these while the regulator refrains from putting pressure to initiate a rating system for corporate governance.

Basel II and CG

Basel II is the second of the Basel Accords recommended on banking laws and regulations issued by the Basel Committee on Banking Supervision. The purpose of Basel II is to create an international standard that banking regulators can use when creating regulations about how much capital banks need to put aside to guard against the types of financial and operational risks (these terms are explained in later sections) banks face. These international standards can help protect the international financial system from the types of problems that might arise should a major bank or a series of banks collapse.

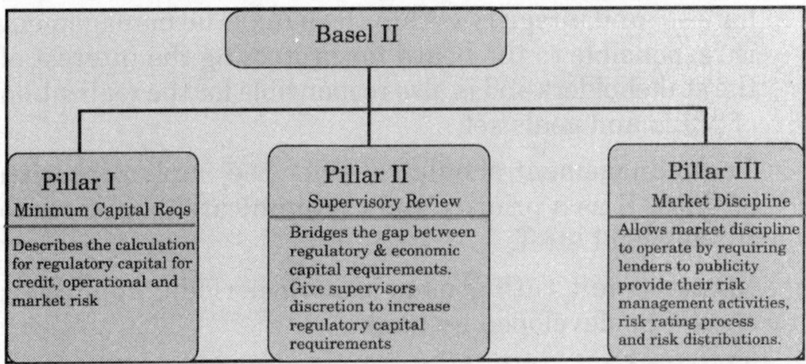

All banks have to comply with Basel II effective from April 1, 2009. Banks' CRAR will have to be at least 8 per cent (as per Basel norms) and 9 per cent (as per RBI norms); banks will also have to maintain minimum Tier I capital to 6 per cent. At present, all banks comply with the Basel II norms; however, there is a tear that its credit growth is to be maintained or it increases, then capital adequacy ratio to several public sector banks will be pushed down. The RBI had stated that Tier I capital to banks should be minimum 6 per cent with effect from March 31, 2010.

The key governance principles that would be relevant to banks have been enumerated in the accord Basel II has listed several principles. Some of them are:

- The board of directors will be composed of people of good character and integrity with expertise knowledge in areas such as law, accounting, banking and risk management.
- Board will ensure that equal treatment is given to all shareholders.
- The board will define the code of conduct for its management and staff.
- The board has the responsibility to finalize the investment plans.
- It will ensure that internal auditors and external auditors are independent.
- The management should promote a culture of trust, honesty and integrity within the bank. The management is responsible to the board for protecting the interest of the stakeholders and is also responsible for the realization of plans and goals set.
- The management should consider the implementation of Basel II as a priority and communicate its process to the relevant staff.
- Proper credit rating models with periodic appraisals should be developed by bank.
- The regulators of the banks should evaluate and approve the ownership structure, organizational structure, business proposals, additions to the board and top management etc.

Finding

In all the regards the big banks (read PSB and large private banks) will have the marked advantage over the small and medium sized banks. This might lead to considerable level of consolidation in the Indian Banking Industry.

An area of relaxation is in the case of private banks which are allowed to access capital from foreign sources up to 74 per cent with no single entity allowed to have an FDI of above 10 per cent. This is leading to foreign firms having substantial stake in Indian private banks.

Indian banks are far behind their foreign counterparts in disclosing information to the public. In the wake of increased competition from foreign banks, disclosure norms can serve to be important differentiating factor to attract and retain big corporate clients.

Basel II in spite of its stringent rules for Capital adequacy provides opportunity for the Indian banks to significantly reduce their credit risk weights and reduce the required regulatory capital.

Conclusion

In the years to come, the Indian financial system will grow not only in size but also in complexity as the forces of competition gain further momentum and financial markets acquire greater depth. There is an assurance that the policy environment will remain supportive of healthy growth and development with accent on more operational flexibility as well as greater prudential regulation and supervision. The real success of our financial sector reforms will however depend primarily on the organisational effectiveness of the banks, for which initiatives will have to come from the banks themselves. With elements of good corporate governance, sound investment policy, appropriate internal control systems, better credit risk management, focus on newly-emerging business areas like micro finance, commitment to better customer service, adequate automation and proactive policies on house-keeping issues, banks will definitely be able to grapple with these challenges and convert them into opportunities.

References

1. Mails, Andreas (2005), Corporate Governance Failures: To What Extent is Parmalat a Particularly Italian Case?
2. Mc Conomy B. and M. Bujaki (2000): “Corporate Governance”, *CMA Management*, Vol. 74,No. 8, pp.10-13.
3. Mohanty P. (2003), “Institutional Investors and Corporate Governance in India” National Stock Exchange Research papers # 42.

4. Mukherjee-Reed A (2002), "Corporate Governance Reforms in India", *Journal of Business Ethics,* Vol. 37, No. 3, pp. 249-268.
5. Millstein, Ira M. (1992), "Corporate Governance, Today and Tomorrow: The Thoughts of Seven Leading Players" Investor Responsibility Research Centre.
6. Narain L., *Principles and Practice of Public Enterprise Management*, S. Chand and Co. 1994.
7. Nachane D. M. and Saibal Ghosh (2001), "Off Balance Sheet Activities in Banking", In Sen R. K. and Chatterjee B (Eds.) *India 2001: Agenda for the 21st Century* (Essays in Honour of P. R. Brahmananda), Deep and Deep Publications, New Delhi.
8. Nippani S. and Washer K. M. (2005), "IBBEA Implementation and the Relative Profitability of Small Banks", *Mid-American Journal of Business,* Fall, Vol. 20, No. 2, pp.19-23.
9. N. R. Narayana Murthy Committee on Corporate Governance (2003).
10. OECD Principle of Corporate Governance (1999 & 2004).
11. OECD (1999), Principles of Corporate Governance Working Paper of Meeting of the OECD Council at Ministerial Level 1999.
12. Oman, C.P. (2001), "Corporate Governance and National Development", OECD Development Centre Technical Papers, Number 180.
13. Raju Satya R. (2003) "Corporate Governance in Selected Organization" *Productivity,* Vol. 43, No. 4, pp.579-586.
14. Rajan R. and Zingales L. (2000b), "The Governance of the New Enterprise" Working Paper, University of Chicago.
15. Raju, R.S. (2003),"Corporate Governance in Selected Organization", *Productivity*, Vol. 43,No.4, pp -579-586.

4

Corporate Governance in Indian Financial Institutions

Theories and Practices

Prof. Sanjay Kanti Das

ABSTRACT

It has been realized that Corporate Governance is vital for better management of any organization. Financial reporting and disclosure of any information are the key factors of corporate governance. Financial institutions are no exceptions and there has been increasing demand for transparency in functioning of these Institutions in view of several scams.

In this paper a modest effort is made to discuss the reporting pattern of India's thirteen financial institutions namely SBI, IDBI, SIDBI, IFCI, NABARD, PNB, UBI, BOB, BOI, LICI, KMB, NHB and HDFC. Top Six commercial banks namely SBI, BOB, PNB, KMB, UBI and BOI, five developments Banks viz. SIDBI, IFCI, HDFC, IDBI, NHB, and NABARD, and one Insurance Company are selected under study .The rationale for selection of these institutes is that being incorporated organizations, they should have same Corporate Governance standards. In view of transparency in functioning, the different committees has a vital role to play. Six parameters have been chosen for comparison of various corporate governance practices in all these thirteen financial institutions namely, company's philosophy on Corporate Governance, Formation of Board of Directors, Composition of Board of Directors, Particulars of Director's, Organizational Committees, and Additional Information supplied in CG report or in the Annual report. Moreover, this paper also highlights the regulatory rules applicable to Public sector banks; co-operative banks, NBFC's and insurance company.

Finally, it is observed that HDFC and PNB are the two financial institutions leading top in the effective CG practices and HDFC leads at the top.

Introduction

Indian economy itself is in the take-off stage with the growth rates averaging in excess of 8 per cent for the past few years, a stock market that has risen over three-fold in as many years and a steady inflow of foreign investment. The long term sustainability of the Indian economy 'success' story depends critically on the state of corporate governance in the country.

The Indian legal system is built on English Common Law and provides one of the highest levels of investor protection in the world.[1] India has a Shareholder Rights Index of 5 (out of a maximum possible of 6), the highest in the rankings presented by Rafael La Porta, Florencio Lopez-de-Silanes, Andrei Shleifer, and Rob Vishny in their 1998 study.[2] In the terms of Creditors Rights, the Indian legal system also seems to provide excellent protection for lenders, according to the La Porta, et al., (1998). On the corruption dimension, India has been ranked 72nd out of 180 countries in the Corruption Index 2007, published by Transparency International. Red tape and regulations are among the main draw backs for business and foreign investment in India, leading to its latest ranking of 120 out of 178 in the World Bank's Doing Business 2008 publication.[3] It also gives India an Investor Protection Score of 6, ahead of each of the other BRIC (Brazil, Russia,

India, and China) countries. In comparing the regulatory powers and performance of the SEBI with those of Securities and Exchange Commission in the US, Suchismita Bose concludes that while the scope of Indian securities laws are quite pervasive, there are significant problems in enforcing compliance, particularly in areas like Price manipulation and insider trading.[4]

Economic growth and development of any country depends upon a well-knit financial system. It comprises a set of sub-systems of financial institutions, financial markets, financial instruments and services which help in the formation of capital. One of the major components of Indian Financial System is the Indian Financial Institution and it is subject to the control of the RBI. Indian Financial Institutions are enriched with the presence of both banking and non-banking financial institutions namely Commercial Banks, Co-operative Banks, RRB's, Development Banks, Insurance and Investment Institutions including Non-Banking Financial Institutions. In fact, Indian Financial system is strong, broad based, diversified and also reached on the stage of 'take off'.

Ensuring effective governance in financial sector is *sine qua non* for any economy's growth and development. It assumes more significance because of its greater dominance as well as the magnitude of repercussions on the economy, in case of their failure. Special emphasis is given to this sector because of the unique character of financial intermediaries and the added complexity of standard governance problems among financial institutions. The banking sector in general, is highly sensitized to public scrutiny and is more vulnerable to the risk of attracting adverse publicity through failings in governance and stakeholder relationships. It is a special sub-set of CG with much of its management obligations enshrined in law or regulatory codes. In the light of the above statement governance issues in banks, more particularly in PSBs is assumed immense significance, but unfortunately these are less discussed and deliberated. Although the primary reason identified to it is the prevalent of govt. ownership across the institutions, another important reason can be attributed to the multiplicity of regulatory and supervisory legislations. For instance in India there are five legislations e.g. RBI Act, SBI Act, Bank Nationalization Act, Banking Regulation Act and Companies Act, govern the banking sector. Because of this multiplicity of Acts and their enforcing agencies i.e. RBI and GoI, any concrete form of principles on bank governance is yet to emerge.

Corporate Governance in Search for a Suitable Definition

Corporate governance is traditionally defined as the system of laws, regulations and practices, which will promote enterprise, accelerate performance and ensure accountability. It stimulates for effectiveness in the performance and operations of a corporate. The effectiveness, in today's parlance, mean that business is run in a manner to enhance stakeholders' value, skewing radically from established enhancement of shareholders' value only and moving towards stakeholders' value maximization.

Corporate Governance for the company means achieving high level of accountability, efficiency, responsibility and fairness in all areas of operation.

"Corporate Governance deals with laws, procedure, practices and implies rules that determine a company's ability to take managerial decision vis a vis its claimants—in particular, its shareholders, creditors, customers and the state" (Bajaj Committee as appointed by CII). "Corporate Governance is concerned with holding the balance between economic and social goals and between individual and communal goals. The corporate governance framework is there to encourage the efficient use of resources and equally to require accountability for the stewardship of those resources. The aim is to align as nearly as possible the interests of individuals, corporations and society" - Sir Adrian Cadbury in 'Global Corporate Governance Forum', World Bank, 2000.

The OECD Principles of Corporate Governance States: "Corporate governance involves a set of relationships between a company's management, its board, its shareholders and other stakeholders. Corporate governance also provides the structure through which the objectives of the company are set, and the means of attaining those objectives and monitoring performance are determined."

Corporate governance is about "the whole set of legal, cultural, and institutional arrangements that determine what public corporations can do, who controls them, how that control is exercised, and how the risks and return from the activities they undertake are allocated."- Margaret Blair, Ownership and Control: Rethinking Corporate Governance for the Twenty-First Century.[5]

"Corporate governance is about how suppliers of capital get managers to return profits, make sure managers do not misuse the capital by investing in bad projects, and how shareholders and creditors monitor managers." -American Management Association.

"Corporate governance is the relationship between corporate managers, directors and the providers of equity, people and institutions who save and invest their capital to earn a return. It ensures that the board of directors is accountable for the pursuit of corporate objectives and that the corporation itself conforms to the law and regulations."- International Chamber of Commerce. [6]

"Corporate governance is the system by which companies are directed and managed. It influences how the objectives of the company are set and achieved, how risk is monitored and assessed, and how performance is optimized. Good corporate governance structures encourage companies to create value (through enterpreneurism, innovation, development and exploration) and provide accountability and control systems commensurate with the risks involved." ASX Principles of Good Corporate Governance and Best Practices Recommendations.[7]

Thus, Corporate Governance practices ensure and promote corporate fairness, transparency and accountability. It is the system through which business corporations are directed and controlled. The corporate governance structure specifies the distribution of rights and responsibility among different participants in the corporation, such as, the board, the managers, shareholders and other stakeholders and spells out the rules and procedures for making decisions on corporate affairs.

Corporate Governance on International Perspectives

International Scenario: At A Glance

Year	*Name of Committee / Body*	*Areas / Aspects Covered*
1992	Sir Adrian Cadbury Committee, UK	Financial Aspects of Corporate Governance
1994	Mervyn E . King's Committee , South Africa	Corporate Governance
1995	Greenbury Committee, UK	Directors' Remuneration
1998	Hampel Committee, UK	Combine Code of Best Practices
1999	Blue Ribbon Committee, US	Improving the Effectiveness of Corporate Audit Committees
1999	OECD	Principles of Corporate Governance
1999	CACG	Principles for Corporate
		Governance in Commonwealth
2003	Derek Higgs Committee, UK	Review of role of effectiveness of Non-executive Directors
2003	ASX Corporate Governance Council, Australia	Principles of Good Corporate Governance and Best Practice Recommendations

Source: Economica India Info Services, cited from 'The Regulatory Norms of Corporate Governance in India'.

The real genesis of the corporate governance lies in the business scams and failures. The Junk Bond Fiasco in USA and the failure of Maxwell, BCCI and Polypeck in UK resulted in the Treadway Committee in USA and the Cadbury Committee in UK on corporate governance. A number of committees were set up to look into various aspects of corporate governance, which included Sir Adrain Cadbury Committee (1992), Greenbury Committee (1995), Hampel Committee (1998), Blue Ribbon Committee (1999), OECD Principles of Corporate Governance (1999) etc. across the globe.

Corporate Governance on Indian Perspectives

Corporate governance in India is evident from the various legal and regulatory frameworks and Committees set relating to corporate functioning comprising of the following:

- Companies Act, 1956
- Monopolies and Restrictive Trade Practices Act, 1969 (replaced by new Competition Law)
- Foreign Exchange Management Act, 2000
- Securities and Exchange Board of India Act, 1992
- Securities Contract Regulation Act, 1956
- The Depositories Act, 1996
- Arbitration and Conciliation Act, 1996
- SEBI Code on Corporate Governance
- CII Code of desirable corporate governance (1998)
- UTI code of governance (1999)
- Kumar Mangalam Birla Committee on Corporate Governance (2000)
- Naresh Chandra Committee (2002)
- N.R. Narayanamurthy Committee (SEBI-2003)

One of the sweeping changes in Indian legislation was the introduction of Clause 49 of the Standard Listing Agreement by SEBI incorporating most of the suggestions of the Kumar Mangalam Birla Committee's report. This was followed by the constitution of N.R. Narayanamurthy Committee by SEBI in 2002 to further analyze Clause 49 of the Standard Listing Agreement that has been amended with the recommendations of the committee's report. Recent amendments to Clause 49 of the Listing Agreement SEBI have announced a complete revision of Clause 49 in the listing agreement of stock exchanges vide circular dated October 29, 2004.

Indian Scenario: At A Glance

Year	*Name of Committee / Body*	*Areas / Aspects Covered*
1998	Confederation of Indian Industry (CII) — Desirable Corporate Governance –A Code	Protection of investor interest, Promotion of transparency, Building international standards in terms of disclosure of information
May 1999	Report of the Committee (Kumar Manglam Birla) on Corporate Governance (SEBI, May 7, 1999)	Responsibilities and obligations of the board and the management in instituting the systems for good corporate governance. Disclosures to be made mandatory and to be published in the annual report.
Nov. 2000	Report of the Task Force on Corporate Excellence through Governance	Corporate Governance in India: A status report Best Practices in Corporate Governance: An Indian and International Position Review Corporate Citizenship and Social Responsiveness Legislation, Regulation and Voluntary Initiatives: Recommendations relating to Corporate Governance matters Proposal for setting up a Centre for Corporate Excellence.
March 2001	RBI – Report of the Advisory Group on Corporate Governance: Standing Committee on International Financial Standards and Code	The comparison of the status of corporate governance in India vis a vis the internationally recognized best standards.
April, 2002	RBI – Report of the Consultative Group of Directors of Banks/Financial Institutions	Supervisory Role of Board of Banks and Financial Institutions Feedback on the functioning of the boards vis a vis compliance, transparency, disclosures, audit committee etc.

December 2002	Report of the Committee (Naresh Chandra) on Corporate Audit and Governance	The statuary auditor company relationship, rotation of statutory audit firms/partners, procedure for appointment of auditors and determination of audit fees, true and fair statement of financial affairs of companies.
February 2003	N. R. Narayan Murthy – SEBI report on Corporate Governance	Audit Committees, Audit Reports, Independent Directors, Risk Management. Directorships and Financial Disclosures.
July, 2003	Naresh Chandra Committee II: Report of the committee on regulation of private companies and partnerships	The Companies Act, 1956, The Indian Partnership Act, 1932
November, 2009	Recommendations for voluntary adoption, Report of the CII Task Force on CG, Chaired by Naresh Chandra	The report is structured according to the different elements of corporate governance: • Non-executive and independent directors • Committees of the board • Significant related party transactions • Independence of Auditors • Rotation of Audit Partners • Legal and regulatory standards • Effective and credible enforcement • Institutional investors • Media

(Contd...)

Year	*Name of Committee / Body*	*Areas / Aspects Covered*
December 2009	CG Voluntary Guidelines Ministry of Corporate Affairs, Government of India.	The report is structured according to the different elements of corporate governance: • Board of Directors • Responsibilities of the Board • Audit Committee of Board • Auditors • Secretarial Audit • Institution of mechanism for Whistle Blowing

Source: Economica India Info Services, cited from 'The Regulatory Norms of Corporate Governance in India'.

This circular supersedes all other earlier circulars issued by SEBI on Clause 49 of the Listing Agreement. SEBI has further extended the date for ensuring compliance with the revised Clause 49 up to December 31, 2005 vide circular no. SEBI/CFD/DIL/CG/1/2005/29/3 dated March 29, 2005.

Significance of Corporate Governance

No matter what view of the corporate objective is taken, effective governance ensures that boards and managers are accountable for pursuing it. The role of effective corporate governance is of immense significance for the society as whole.[8] At first place it promotes the efficient use of scarce resources both within the organization and the economy. Secondly, it makes the resources flow to those sectors or entities where there are efficient production of goods and services and the return is adequate enough to satisfy the demands of stakeholders. Thirdly, it provides a broad mechanism of choosing the best managers to administer the scarce resources. Fourthly, it helps the mangers to remain focused on improving performance, making sure that they are replaced when they fail to do so. Fifthly, it pressurizes the organization to comply with the laws, regulations and expectations of society and last but not the least it assists the supervisors to regulate the entire economic sector without partiality and nepotism.

The importance of the issue of Corporate Governance in banks and other financial institutions is just like any other organization. As a result of which, the primary requirements of corporate Governance apply to them as any other incorporated entity. The fact is reflected that banks forms an integral part of the economy of the country, and any failure in a bank might have a direct bearing on the financial health of the country. Banks help in chanelising the people's saving that acts as a multiplier on driving the economy forward. The second important driver of a good Corporate Governance stems from their funding patterns. The stakeholders in banks, (mainly the depositors and lenders) have a rightful claim of accountability from the banks and their boards. The third important element in the Corporate Governance structure relates to the control function. Finally, failing to comply with stipulated norms can be one of the challenging issues of Corporate Governance framework. With Banks being under intense watch of the Central Bank as well as other regulatory bodies, it is a common observation, that most failures (crashes) in banks have occurred due to compliance failure situations.[9]

Importance of implementing modern corporate governance standards is conditioned by the global tendency to consolidation in the banking sector and a need in further capitalization. Best Corporate Governance practices will enable banks to:

- Increase efficiency of their activities and minimize risks;
- Get an easier access to capital markets and decrease the cost of capital;
- Increase growth rate;
- Attract strategic investors;
- Improve the standards of lending;
- Protect the rights of minority shareholder and other counterparts;
- Strengthen their reputation and raise the level of investors and clients' trust.

Principles of Corporate Governance

Key elements of good corporate governance principles include honesty, trust and integrity, openness, performance orientation, responsibility and accountability, mutual respect, and commitment to the organization. The essence of good governance depends on how directors and management develop a model of governance that aligns the values of the corporate participants and then evaluate this model periodically for its effectiveness. In particular, senior executives should conduct themselves honestly and ethically, especially concerning actual or apparent conflicts of interest, and disclosure in financial reports. Some commonly accepted principles of Corporate Governance includes:

Rights and equitable treatment of shareholders: Organizations should respect the rights of shareholders and help shareholders to exercise those rights. They can help shareholders exercise their rights by effectively communicating information that is understandable and accessible and encouraging shareholders to participate in general meetings.

Interests of other stakeholders: Organizations should recognize that they have legal and other obligations to all legitimate stakeholders.

Role and responsibilities of the board: The board needs a range of skills and understanding to be able to deal with various business issues and have the ability to review and challenge management performance. It needs to be of sufficient size and have an appropriate level of commitment to fulfill its responsibilities and duties. There are issues about the appropriate mix of executive and non-executive directors. The key roles of chairperson and CEO should not be held by the same person.

Integrity and ethical behavior: Ethical and responsible decision making is not only important for public relations, but it is also a necessary element in risk management. Organizations should develop a code of conduct for their directors and executives that promotes ethical and responsible decision-making.

Disclosure and transparency: Organizations should clarify and make publicly known the roles and responsibilities of board and management to provide shareholders with a level of accountability. They should also implement procedures to independently verify and safeguard the integrity of the company's financial reporting. Disclosure of material matters concerning the organization should be timely and balanced to ensure that all investors have access to clear, factual information.

Corporate Governance in Indian Public Financial Institutions

In India, the public sector banks are functioning with a safe wall around them provided by government ownership. The perception of the government owing the liability of bank failure prevails and attention to know the strength does not receive importance. Government being the controlling shareholder yields special influence on governance of public financial institutions as it selects almost all directors in the case of unlisted public financial institutions. On the contrary, being a government organization, their operations are regulated by rules and procedures prescribed by Ministry of Finance and by RBI, hence board does not have any scope to exercise its powers.

Government ownership is one of the primary issues that can have a direct impact on the quality of Corporate Governance. In public sector banks, the rights of the private shareholders are considerably curtailed as their approval is not required for paying dividend or formalizing the annual accounts. Several issues pertaining to the composition of the board has also plagued the Corporate Governance framework. These issues relate to the appointment of directors, fixing of remuneration, professional qualification required etc.

The objective of the government as the major stakeholder of the public sector banks has been to balance the constraints imposed by its accountability to parliament on behalf of these institutions, with the statutory mandate to nominate the board of these institutions in such a manner as to ensure effective management.

Corporate Governance and Non-Banking Financial Companies

Corporate Governance is the key to protecting the interests of the stake-holders in the corporate sector. Its universal applicability has no exception to the Non-Banking Financial Companies (NBFCs) which too are essentially corporate entities. Listed NBFCs which are required to adhere to listing agreement and rules framed by SEBI on Corporate Governance are already required to comply with SEBI prescriptions on Corporate Governance. In order to enable NBFCs to adopt best practices and greater transparency in their operations following guidelines.[10] are proposed for consideration of the Board of Directors of all deposit taking NBFCs with deposit size of Rs. 20 crore and above and all non-deposit taking NBFCs with asset size of Rs. 100 crore and above (NBFC-ND-SI) namely, (i) Constitution of Audit Committee, (ii) Constitution of Nomination Committee, (iii) Constitution of Risk Management Committee, (iv) Disclosure and transparency.

Corporate Governance and Co-operative Bank

Corporate Governance especially in the co-operative sector has come into sharp focus because a large number of co-operative banks in India, both in urban and rural areas, have experienced grave problems in recent times which have in a way threatened the profile and identity of the entire co-operative system. These problems include mismanagement, financial crisis, poor investment decisions and the growing distance between members and their co-operative society.

Co-operatives are organized groups of people and jointly managed and democratically controlled enterprises. They exist to serve their members and depositors and produce benefits for them. Co-operative corporate governance is therefore about ensuring co-operative relevance and performance by connecting members, management and the employees to the policy, strategy and decision-making processes.

Corporate Governance and Insurance Companies

The Corporate Governance framework should clearly define the roles and responsibilities and accountability within an organization with built-in checks and balances. The importance of Corporate Governance has received emphasis in recent times since poor governance and weak internal controls have been associated with major corporate failures including insurance companies. In the insurance sector, the regulatory responsibility to protect the interests of the policyholders demands that the insurers have in place, good governance practices for maintenance of solvency, sound long term investment policy and assumption of underwriting risks on a prudential basis.

The Insurance Regulatory and Development Authority (IRDA) has outlined in general terms, governance responsibilities of the Board in the management of the insurance functions under various Regulations notified by it covering different operational areas.

The Insurance Company can establish several committees to undertake specific functions depending on the size and level of the complexity of the operations. Typically, the committees that assist the Board are Audit Committee, Risk Management Committee, Nominations Committee, Remuneration Committee, Investment Committee and Asset-Liability Management Committee. However, the Authority advises insurers that it is mandatory to establish Audit; Investment; Risk Management: Policyholder Protection; and Asset Liability Management (in case of life insurers) Committees that have a critical role in strengthening the control environment in the company.

Problems of Corporate Governance in Banks in India

The banking sector in general, is highly sensitized to public scrutiny and is more vulnerable to the risk of attracting adverse publicity through failings in governance and stakeholder relationships. It is a special sub-set of CG with much of its management obligations enshrined in law or regulatory codes. In the light of the above statement governance issues in banks, more particularly in PSBs assume immense significance, but unfortunately these are less discussed and deliberated. Although the primary reason identified to it is the prevalent of govt. ownership across the institutions, another important reason can be attributed to the multiplicity of regulatory and supervisory legislations. For instance, in India there are 5 legislations e.g. RBI Act, SBI Act, Bank Nationalization Act, Banking Regulation Act and Companies Act, govern the banking sector. Because of this multiplicity of Acts and their enforcing agencies i.e. RBI and GoI, any concrete form of principles on bank governance is yet to emerge.

Policy Framework of CG in Indian Banking

Committee Recommendations and Implementation

The global policy formulation on this issue can be traced to the industrialized countries. Blue Ribbon Commission of US, Cadbury Committee from UK, and many stock exchanges around the world started flouting governance principles and the World Bank and OECD tried to give all the principles in a comprehensive framework. India started its ground work for CG principle implementation after many years of the implementation of Codes of Best Practices developed by the Cadbury Committee, 1991. Considerable attention has been given to CG in India in recent years. In addition to the Advisory Group chaired by Dr. R.H. Patil (RBI, 2001) and Consultative Group of Directors of Banks/Financial Institutions (Ganguly Group, RBI, 2002), several official committees have already gone into the issues relating to CG and have given their reports. These include the Committee chaired by Shri Kumar Mangalam Birla (SEBI, 1999), the Task Force on Corporate Excellence through Governance (GOI, 2000), Naresh Chandra Committee on Corporate Audit and Governance (SEBI, 2002), Naresh Chandra Committee-II on Regulation of Private Companies and Partnership (GOI, 2003) and Narayana Murthy Committee on Corporate Governance (SEBI, 2003). Mangalam Committee has gone into disclosure norms for other documents (SEBI, 2004) that would also contribute towards improving CG in the country. Preceding these official committees, the industry association, CII, had itself provided a Code in 1998 /2009. Governance principle formulation exclusively for banking came little late.

Although some regulations were issued by the Basel Committee on Banking Supervision (BCBS) way back in 1988, these were not considered as exclusive CG principles. The Basel banking regulations issued in 1999, however, brought an array of principles over a broad spectrum of banking activities. The OECD principles also tried to fulfill some of the requirements of banking industry. Keeping in view the widely accepted Basel recommendations in the background many countries framed their own set of governance principles for their banking industries. For Indian banking, the RBI has taken the sole responsibility of framing policy in this regard.

Looking at the developments of governance practices and its implementations in India, it is found that till the year 2002 most of them were at recommendatory stage. Most of the suggestions given by the Advisory Group (2001) and Ganguly Committee (2002) were implemented during and after the year 2002. [Annexure I]

Objective of the Study

The basic objective of this study is to compare and evaluate different Corporate Governance procedures followed by Indian Public Financial Institutions namely SBI, IDBI, SIDBI, IFCI, NABARD, PNB, UBI, BOB, BOI, LICI, KMB, NHB and HDFC. Top six commercial banks namely SBI, BOB, PNB, KMB UBI & BOI, five developments banks viz. SIDBI, IFCI, HDFC, IDBI, NHB, and NABARD, and one Insurance Company are selected under study. The rationale for selection of these institutions is that being incorporated organisations, they should have same Corporate Governance standards. These thirteen institutions have been compared on the basis of company's philosophy on corporate governance, requirement and number of Director's on Board, various committees formed for effective Corporate Governance and additional information as disclosed in their Corporate Governance Report in annual report of year 2009-10.

Analysis of Different Parameters of Corporate Governance

Six parameters have been chosen for comparison of various corporate governance practices in SBI, IDBI, SIDBI,

IFCI, NABARD, PNB, UBI, BOB, BOI, LICI, KMB, NHB and HDFC namely:

1. Company's Philosophy on Corporate Governance
2. Formation of Board of Directors
3. Composition of Board of Directors
4. Particulars of Director's
5. Committees
6. Additional Information

1. Company's Philosophy on Corporate Governance

All the thirteen financial institutions follow different philosophy on corporate governance. But all concentrate on basic philosophy of transparency and accountability. SBI has additional philosophy of integrity in communication technique. HDFC has assured its shareholders that there is well performing management to take care of their assets. Financial institutions like SBI, IBDI, LICI, PNB, KMB and NHB narrated corporate governance as means to protect the interest of shareholders/stakeholders. The financial institutions like BOB and BOI made a commitment to follow the best international practices and assure high disclosure standards and transparency. The details of philosophy of individual institutions are as categorically explained in Table 4.1.

2. Formation of Board of Directors

Composition of Board of all the thirteen financial institutions under study is constituted according to the Act under which these organisations are incorporated. The information disclosed under this category is compiled in Table 4.2. Financial institutions like BOB, BOI and NABARD is having 12 members each on its Board of Directors. The financial institutions like NHB, IFCI and HFDC has 11 members on its Board, while KMB has 9 members in its Board, UBI has only 7 members on its Board of Directors. The SBI and PNB are the leader in the group under study having 13 members each on their Board of Directors.

3. Composition of Board of Directors

The composition of Executive Directors and Non-executive Directors along with the number of independent and nominee directors of all the thirteen financial institutions under study are shown in Table 4.3. All the thirteen financial institutions under study except SIDBI, LICI and NHB does not clearly mention in their Annual Report about the composition of executive, non-executive and independent directors which is against the recommendation of Ganguly Committee and Advisory Committee on Corporate Governance. SIDBI has 15 numbers of directors on its board but does not disclose the clear sub-division about the number of non-executive, executive and independent directors. Similarly, LICI and NHB have 10 numbers and 11 numbers of directors respectively on its Board but do not disclose the clear sub-division about the number of non-executive, executive and independent directors. IDBI has six independent directors out of 10 directors on the Board including 8 non-executive directors. IFCI has 9 numbers of non-executive directors out of 11 directors, but they do not disclose about the number of independent directors. SBI and PNB are the leaders in this study group in respect of appointing non-executive directors (10 non-executive directors out of 13 directors) but do not disclose the number of independent directors. LICI have 10 directors on its board having both executive, non-executive directors and independent directors but does not disclose the clear composition of the Board about executive, non-executive directors and independent directors. HDFC has 9 non-executive directors out of its 11 directors and also disclose the number of independent directors (5 independent directors out of 11 directors). BOB and BOI have equal number of directors i.e. 12 directors on their Boards and equal number of representation of non-executive directors but BOB does not disclose the number of independent directors on the Board. UBI and KMB have also mentions the number of executive and non-executive directors and also having requisite number of independent directors. Further, the financial institutions like SIDBI, LICI, NHB and NABARD have disclosed the number of nominee directors on their Boards. Lastly, KMB have appointed non-executive directors as its chairman of the Board and also fulfilled the regulatory norms regarding the appointment of at least half of the Board (5 out of 9 as independent directors) as independent directors.

4. Particulars of Director's

In this paper, the particulars of directors are studied under three distinct heads viz. information about the salary and sitting fees of directors, brief resume of directors and information about the attendance of directors in the Board / committee meetings. All these information are tabulated in the Table 4.4 SIDBI, UBI, NHB and NABARD do not disclose brief information about the salary and sitting fees of the directors. Except these all other financial institutions under study disclose the amount or provision relating to salary and sitting fees payable to non-executive directors. Some of the institutions also mentioned the government rules regarding the salary and perquisites to be paid to the directors/ Managing directors and do not mention the exact amount to be paid to directors as salary and perquisites.

SBI mention only the brief resume of non-executive directors. KMB and HDFC mention the brief resume of all the existing directors in their Annual Reports. LICI, IFCI, IDBI, and SIDBI do not disclose the brief resume of their directors. NABARD, PNB, BOB, BOI, UBI and NHB also do not disclose the brief resume of their existing directors but only newly appointed director's resume in mentioned in their Annual Reports.

It is also observed that almost all the financial institutions except SIDBI, LICI, and NHB has disclosed the information about the names of director's, their directorship, Chairmanship, or membership in other company and other committees of the institution and also their attendance on the meetings either on Board or committee meetings. It is observed that in all most all financial institutions except

HDFC, IFCI, BOB and UBI, the regulations in respect of directorship in other company or chairmanship in the other committee's of the institutions or membership in other committees of the institutions are not strictly followed. (see Table 4.6 Point 20, Multiple Board Seats). SBI mentioned all these information as a separate annexure while others (except SIDBI, LICI, and NHB) disclosed the fact in the corporate governance report. Further, NHB and LICI only disclose the directorship and committee membership of board member but does not disclose their attendance on either board or committee meetings. SIDBI disclose only the total number of board meeting held during the year.

5. Committees

Cadbury Committee (UK,1992) has prescribed three committees namely Audit Committee, Remuneration Committee and Nomination Committee. In India, no statutory requirement is placed for the number of committees to be framed by any statutory organization except Clause 49 of Listing Agreement (Birla Committee-1999) which mandates Audit Committee, Remuneration Committee and Shareholders Committee. All the thirteen financial institutions under study constituted a number of committees for Corporate Governance. The details of committees constituted by these institutions are depicted in the Table 4.5.

SBI has framed eight (8) committees except nomination committee. SIDBI has constituted seven (7) major committees except nomination committee, remuneration committee and shareholder's committee. IDBI constituted eight (8) committees including all mandatory committees. LICI has also set up four (4) committees except audit committee, nomination committee, shareholder's committee and remuneration committee. HDFC has not constituted remuneration committee though they have constituted nine (9) major committees. UBI has constituted eight (8) committees except nomination committee. BOI have also constituted three (3) committees except nomination and remuneration committees. Similarly, NHB and NABARD have also failed to constitute remuneration committee, nomination committee and shareholders committee. In fact, PNB has constituted the largest number of committees i.e. 16 committees followed has by KMB which framed 14 committees and BOB constituted has 10 committees and both have fulfilled the regulatory norms regarding the formation of different committees.

6. Additional Information

Comparison has been made on the additional information about AGM of Shareholders, Market Price Data, Distribution pattern of Shareholders, Address for Correspondence, Details of Dematerialization etc. as disclosed in the corporate governance report and the Annual Reports of these thirteen financial institutions under study and shown in the Table 4.6.

RBI instructed all the banks and financial institutions to include separate section on CG on their Annual Reports. Most of the financial institutions under study made a separate section on CG in their Annual Reports except LICI, BOI and NABARD. All most all the financial institutions under study except LICI, BOI, SIDBI and NABARD do not provide any separate section on the CG. But all of them either incorporated a separate section on CG in their Annual Reports or included a paragraph about CG on their Director's reports.

SIDBI, LICI, NHB and NABARD do not provide any particulars about Annual General Meeting have or shareholder's information in their Report.

It is observed that those financial institutions which are listed in the stock exchanges have disclosed the information about the market price of shares and shareholder's/ stakeholders pattern. Information about details of dematerialization are disclosed by allotment of all the financial institutions except SBI, SIDBI, LICI, KMB, NHB and NABARD. Further, information about the details of employee stock option is also incorporated by some financial institutions like IDBI, IFCI, HDFC and KMB. Except IFCI and HDFC, no financial institutions under study has disclosed the information about the system of review of Chairman on the functioning of different committees. This need to be considered as one of the positive aspects on good corporate governance practices of IFCI and HDFC.

All most all financial institutions under study except SIDBI, LICI, NHB and NABARD specifically have mention the Director's Report and Auditor's Compliance Report on CG and which are duly incorporated as one section in the Annual report. However, in the annual reports of SIDBI, LICI, NHB and NABARD, the facts about CG is also articulated prudently in the Director's/Chairman's Report.

All the commercial Banking institutions including HDFC under study like SBI, KMB, PNB, BOB and BOI has disclosed their maintenance of Basel II norms, while UBI is able to maintain the Basel III norms. Other financial institutions under study (except the earlier specified commercial banks) has not disclosed the matter relating to Basel norms.

All the thirteen financial institutions under study have disclosed both the accounting policies and standards and related party disclosure (AS 18). Every financial institution under study has also disclosed the total number of Board meetings held during the financial year except SIDBI, NHB and NABARD. SBI and KMB are the leading bank in holding Board meetings (10 Board meetings). PNB conducted only three (3) Board meeting during the period of study which is against the regulatory norms regarding number of Board meetings.

Regarding the Multiple Board Seats, HDFC only has declared that none of the members on board who is a member of more than ten committees and chairman of more than five committees. However, after due observation from the CG report and Director's report, it is seen that IFCI, BOI and UBI also maintains the due regulatory norms regarding Multiple Board Seats. SIDBI, NHB and NABARD have not disclosed any information about multiple Board seats. Thus, it is concluded that HDFC is the only financial institution under study which disclosed another positive aspects of good governance.

Another non-mandatory requirement of CG is the Whistle Blower Policy which is duly maintained by all most all the financial institutions under study except SIDBI, IFCI, LICI, NHB and NABARD. In fine, only IFCI and UBI have disclosed the information about the names of directors who are seeking appointment/ reappointment as director/s on the Board, while other financial institutions under study fails to disclose these facts in their annual reports. Lastly, all the financial institutions except SBI, SIDBI, IFCI, LICI, KMB, NHB and NABARD under study also mentioned the fact of external credit rating and some of them also accredited by some specialized external credit rating institutions (Domestic and overseas credit rating agencies). However, BOI and UBI are the voluntary members of BCSBI. BOB and PNB have also awarded with the CG rating.

Key Observations

All the thirteen financial institutions under study have been compared on the basis of institutional philosophy on CG, requirement and number of directors on the Board, formation of different committees and additional information as disclosed in their Reports on CG of the Annual Report for the year 2009-10.

All the financial institutions under study have shown the same philosophy of CG on transparency, accountability and fairness for performance and enhancing the shareholder's value except SIDBI, LICI, UBI and NABARD who remains salient about that aspect of CG in enhancing shareholder's value. HDFC has taken special responsibility to take care of their assets and also emphasized on shareholder's empowerment. SBI emphasized on effective management and control of business through CG. Some financial institutions namely PNB, BOB and BOI also explained the philosophy of CG as the means to develop ethical values in banking business. The PNB also stress on implementing best practices in corporate governance as they believe in full transparency in all their business operations and policies, and Zero tolerance for any malpractices. Thus, PNB is ahead of others followed by HDFC and NABARD has lowers value for CG.

It is also observed that the Board of Directors are appointed in these thirteen financial institutions according to the Act in which they are incorporated. SIDBI is the leader in the group in appointing a large number of directors (15 directors) followed by PNB and SBI having 13 directors each, on the Board, then followed by BOB, BOI and NABARD with 12 directors each on the Board and UBI has the least seven directors on their Board.

It is also seen that non-executive directors are maximum in the Board of SBI and PNB (10 non-executive directors each) followed by IFCI, HDFC, BOB and BOI (9 non-executive directors each) while UBI have only 5 non-executive directors, NHB and SIDBI have not mentioned about the numbers of non-executive directors in the board. Moreover, IDBI, HDFC, BOI, UBI, KMB and NHB have also disclosed the number of independent directors in their Board. The representation of independent directors in the Board of HDFC is large in comparison to others (5 independent directors out of 11 directors on the Board). This is one positive sign of good Corporate Governance practice in HDFC.

All the financial institutions under study except SIDBI, UBI, NHB and NABARD have not provided any information about salary and perquisites paid to chairman/Directors and sitting fees paid to non-executive directors. SBI has disclosed the brief information of only non-executive directors while IDBI, SIDBI, IFCI, LICI, and NHB have not disclosed the brief resume of directors. UBI, BOI, PNB, BOB and NABARD have disclosed only the newly appointed director's profile. Only KMB and HDFC have disclosed brief profile of the entire existing director's and leads top in this parameter followed by SBI and PNB.

PNB, IDBI, SBI, HDFC, IFCI, BOB, BOI, UBI, KMB and NABARD in their Annual Reports have furnished information about their director's attendance on different Board and committee meetings along with their directorship and committee membership. SIDBI, LICI and NHB have not disclosed the aforesaid fact but LICI disclosed the information about directorship and committee membership of Board members.

Regarding the Multiple Board Seats only HDFC has declared that none of the members on board who is a member of more than ten committees and chairman of more than five committees. Hence, only HDFC gets a credit in this context and tops the rank in this segment of CG aspects.

PNB takes the lead by constituting 16 committees for efficient functioning followed by KMB with 14 committees, BOB with 10 committees, HDFC with 9 committees while SBI, IDBI and UBI with 8 committees each and lowest number of committees is constituted by IFCI, BOI and NABARD (3 committees each). Therefore, PNB leads ahead in the formation of committees.

In view of additional information provided in CG/Annual Report, HDFC leads by supplying 19 information out of 21 queries followed by PNB and UBI (18 information), then IFCI and BOB (17 information) and NHB with least 4 types of additional information. Therefore, it is obvious that HDFC takes a lead in supplying additional information.

Conclusion

Thus, it is observed that both HDFC and PNB are in the keen competition in maintaining the best practices with regard to CG practices. The positive aspects of HDFC's CG practices includes Broad Corporate Governance philosophy, requisite and sufficient number of Board members with large representation of independent directors, and disclosure of information relating to profile of existing directors. Another positive aspect of HDFC governance practices is the declaration of multiple Board seats and it is claimed that 'none of the members on board who is a member of more than ten committees and chairman of more than five committees'. Moreover, HDFC supplies 19 additional information out of 21 queries which also signifies the best practices on CG from theirs end. Lastly, it is also reported that the bank maintains CG voluntary guidelines 2009. The bank ensures 'disclosure and transparency' in financial statements as per Section 29 of Banking Regulation Act, 1949; RBI guidelines; Section 49 of the Listing Agreement; Accounting Standards and Guidelines issued by the Institute of Chartered Accountants of India, etc. In addition to the statutory disclosures, the Bank discloses voluntarily additional information by way of Directors' Report about the bank's overall performance, business strategies, products and services, Risk Management etc. The only negative aspect of CG practices which is found in HDFC's Annual Report is the non-constitution of remuneration committee.

The positive aspects of good and effective CG in PNB includes ethical and value based corporate philosophy, large number of Board of Directors, large number of committee for effective functioning. PNB ensures 'disclosure and transparency' in financial statements as per Section 29 of Banking Regulation Act, 1949; RBI guidelines; Section 49 of the Listing Agreement; Accounting Standards and Guidelines issued by the Institute of Chartered Accountants of India, etc. Disclosures as per RBI guidelines & ICAI Accounting Standards (AS) include Segment reporting, Related Party Disclosures, Lending to sensitive sectors, etc. In addition to the statutory disclosures, the Bank discloses voluntarily additional information by way of Directors' Report about the bank's overall performance, business strategies, products and services, Risk Management etc. The bank gives high priority to good Corporate Governance. ICRA Ltd, the rating agency has reaffirmed the CGR 2 rating (on a rating scale of CG R1 to CGR 6, where CGR 1 denotes the highest rating) to the Bank in February 2010, which reflects that PNB has adopted and follows such practices, conventions and codes as would provide its financial stakeholders a high level of assurance on the quality of Corporate Governance. This is the highest rating assigned to a financial institution in India. The Bank has complied with the guidelines of Reserve Bank of India and SEBI on the matters relating to Corporate Governance, which has been examined by the Statutory Central Auditors. The Bank is guided (to the extent possible/applicable) by the acclaimed OECD (Organization for Economic Co-operation and Development) principles of Corporate Governance as far as responsibilities of the Board of Directors, governance infrastructure, rights of shareholders, equitable treatment of shareholders, role of shareholders in governance and disclosures and transparency are concerned. The negative points in respect of CG practices by PNB includes non-discloser of number of independent directors on the Board, lack of information about profile of all the existing directors, less number of Board meetings, and the bank supply only 18 additional information out of 21 specified questions. Thus, it is observed from the above that HDFC takes the lead in Corporate Governance practices because it able to disclose more information in its report than others followed by PNB.

It also seems that all being government organisations except KMB, only provides information which stipulates to requirements of Clause 49 (Birla Committee, 1999) of the Listing Agreement with stock exchanges. Thus government and RBI should prescribe a format for reporting of Corporate Governance for these Public Financial Institutions and Governance Audit should be made compulsory. It is also realized that in Indian Public Financial Corporations, Corporate Governance is still in nascent stage because so far no fixed format have been prescribed for Corporate

Governance Report and various committees have been constituted by Statutory Authorities to suggest best Corporate Governance procedures.

From the perspective of banking industry, corporate governance also includes in its ambit the manner in which their boards of directors govern the business and affairs of individual institutions and their functional relationship with senior management. This is determined by how banks:

- set corporate objectives (including generating economic returns to owners);
- run the day-to-day operations of the business;
- consider the interests of recognized stakeholders i.e., employees, customers, suppliers, supervisors, governments and the community; and
- align corporate activities and behaviors with the expectation that banks will operate in a safe and sound manner, and in compliance with applicable laws and regulations; and of course protect the interests of depositors, which is suprem.

Table 4.1 Company's Philosophy on Corporate Governance

Name of Financial Institutions	*Philosophy on Corporate Governance*
1. SBI	The Bank believes that proper corporate governance facilitates effective management and control of business, which enables the Bank to maintain a high level of business ethics and to optimize the value for all its stakeholders.
2. IDBI	Long term enhancement of all stakeholders value and providing a transparent atmosphere in business dealings. The Bank's policies and practices are not only in line with the statutory requirement but also reflect its commitment to operate in the best interest of its stakeholders.
3. SIDBI	The bank has been following the tenets of business fairness transparency, accountability and responsibility
4. IFCI	Corporate Governance is based on the principle of fairness, equity, transparency, accountability and dissemination of information. It believes in maintaining highest standards of Corporate Governance as a part of its legacy and constitution.
5. LICI	Operational transparency, information sharing, accountability and ensuring dialogue with all the stakeholders in addition to formulation of value-based policies and practices at all levels.
6. HDFC	Best board practices, transparent disclosures and shareholder empowerment are necessary for creating shareholder value. The philosophy on corporate governance is an important tool for shareholder protection and maximization of their long term values.

(Contd...)

7. PNB	Corporate Governance is ensured by the Bank by adhering to high standards of accountability, transparency, social responsiveness, operational efficiencies, best ethical business practices for maximizing the shareholders' value and to protect the interest of all stakeholders besides complying with Regulatory requirement.
8. BOB	The Bank shall continue its endeavor to enhance its shareholders' value by protecting their interest by ensuring performance at all levels, and maximizing returns with optimal use of resources in its pursuit of excellence. The Bank believes in setting high standards of ethical values, transparency and a disciplined approach to achieve excellence in all its sphere of activities. The Bank is also committed to follow the best international practices.
9. BOI	Commitment to ethical practices in the conduct of its business, high disclosure standards and transparency and enhancement shareholders' value are the key of CG. The interrelation between the Board, the executives and other functionaries is so configured as to have distinctly demarcated roles and improved corporate performance.
10.UBI	Corporate governance stands for responsible and value creating management and control of the bank. It believes in high standard of ethical values, transparency and disciplined approach to achieve in all fields of activities.
11. KMB	The Bank believes in adopting and adhering to the best standards of corporate governance to all the stakeholders. Guiding principles of CG includes (i) Appropriate composition, size of the Board and commitment to adequately discharge its responsibilities and duties. (ii) Transparency and independence in the functions of the Board. (iii) Independent verification and assured integrity of financial reporting., (iv) Adequate risk management and Internal Control, (v) Protection of shareholders' rights and priority for investor relations., and vi) Timely and accurate disclosure on all matters concerning operations and performance of the Bank.
12. NHB	The Bank has committed to follow the best practices on corporate governance and has laid down emphasis on the cardinal values of fairness, transparency and accountability for performance at all levels in dealing with its stakeholders.
13. NABARD	Corporate Governance is mandatory and hence incorporated in the Annual Return.

Table 4.2 Formation of the Board

Name of the Financial Institutions	*Formation of the Board*
1. SBI	A Central Board of Directors was constituted as per the provisions of the State Bank of India Act, 1955. There are 16 members of Board, i.e. one Chairman of bank, two MD, and ten other whole time directors. There are four directors nominated by shareholders, five nominated by Central Government and one nominated by RBI. However, there are three executive directors including the Chairman and ten non-executive directors. Number of independent directors is not mentioned in the Annual Report.
2. IDBI	Composition of Board of Directors is provided in IDBI Act, 1964. At present there are ten members on Board of which two are executive directors including Chairman and eight Non Executive Directors and six Independent Directors.
3. SIDBI	The SIDBI Act provides for 15 members B.O.D. comprising Chairman, MD, two directors nominated by G.O.I., four elected by shareholders and rest are nominated by G.O.I. on behalf of various institutions.
4. IFCI	The Board of the Company governed by IFCI Act, consisted of eleven directors, out of whom nine directors were non-executive while one was managing director and chief executive officer and one was whole time director.
5. LICI	The Board is governed by the LICI Act, 1956 and presently having ten directors as both executive directors and non-executive directors. There is the provision of nominee directors and independent directors. But no special mention is made in the annual report about the number of executive, non-executive and independent directors.

(Contd...)

6.HDFC	the composition of the Board of Directors of the Bank is governed by the Companies Act, 1956, the Banking Regulation Act, 1949 and the listing requirements of the Indian Stock Exchanges where the securities issued by the Bank are listed. The Board has strength of eleven directors. Out of which three are executive directors. The Bank has five independent directors and six non-independent directors.
7.PNB	The Board is constituted in accordance with Section 9 (3) of Banking Companies (Acquisition and Transfer of Undertakings) Act, 1970 having 13 directors, of which10 are non-executive and three are executive. No mentions are found in the annual report about the number of independent directors. In the Board, there are three directors appointed by GOI, three directors appointed by Shareholder, one each as officer nominee, GOI nominee, RBI nominee and workmen nominee.
8.BOB	The composition of Board of Directors of the Bank is governed by the provisions of the Banking Regulation Act, 1949, the Banking Companies (Acquisition and Transfer of Undertakings) Act, 1970, as amended and the Nationalized Banks (Management and Miscellaneous Provisions) Scheme, 1970, as amended, There are 12 directors, of them nine are non executive directors and three are executive directors including Chairman. In the Board, there are three directors nominated by GOI, three directors appointed by Shareholder, one each as officer-employee nominee and workmen-employee nominee.
9.BOI	The Bank is constituted under the Banking Companies (Acquisition and Transfer of Undertakings) Act, 1970 as amended from time to time. The general superintendence, direction and management of the affairs and business of the Bank is vested in the Board of Directors presided over by the Chairman and Managing Director. There are 12 directors, of them three are executive directors and five are independent directors. In the Board, there are three directors appointed by Shareholder, one each as workmen employee nominee, GOI nominee, RBI nominee and non-workmen employee nominee.

10. UBI	The board has been constituted in accordance with sec 9(3) of the Banking Companies (Acquisition and Transfer of Undertaking) Act, 1970, and as per the Central Govt Gazette Notification. There are seven Directors in BOD, two executive directors, five non-executive and one independent director only.
11. KMB	The composition of the Board of Directors of the Bank is governed by the Banking Regulation Act, 1949 and Clause 49 of the Listing Agreement. The Board of Directors, comprising a combination of executive and non executive Directors, presently consists of nine members, of who six are non-executive Directors. The Chairman of the Board is a non-executive Director and five out of nine Directors are independent.
12. NHB	The Board of Directors has been constituted in accordance with the provisions of the National Housing Bank Act, 1987 (Central Act No. 53 of 1987). The composition of eleven directors includes four Independent Directors, two nominated by Reserve Bank of India, three officials of the Central Government, and two officials of the State Governments. In the Board, there are two directors appointed by RBI, three Central Govt Officials and two State Govt Officials.
13. NABARD	The Board is governed by NABARD Act, 1982. There is clear bifurcation about mode of Board of Directors appointed, but no mention about the number of dependant and independent directors. There are total 12 Directors in the Board, of them four are executive directors.

Table 4.3 Composition of Board of Directors

Name of the Financial Institutions	*Composition of Board of Directors*
1. SBI	3 executive directors and 10 non-executive directors = 13
2. IDBI	2 executive directors and 8 non executive directors = 10
3. SIDBI	15 directors
4. IFCI	2 executive directors and 9 non-executive directors = 11
5. LICI	10 directors
6. HDFC	3 executive directors and 9 non-executive directors = 11
7. PNB	3 executive directors and 10 non-executive directors = 13
8. BOB	3 executive directors and 9 non executive directors = 12
9. BOI	3 executive directors and 9 non executive directors = 12
10. UBI	2 executive directors and 5 non executive directors = 7
11. KMB	3 executive directors and 6 non –executive directors = 9
12. NHB	11 directors
13. NABARD	4 executive directors and 8 non-executive directors = 12

Table 4.4 Particulars of Director's

Name of Financial Institutions	*Particulars of Director's*
1. SBI	(1) Information about Salary and Perquisites paid to Chairman and Managing Director is given and Sitting Fees paid to other Directors is also mentioned. (2) Brief resume of only non-executive Director is given. (3) Table regarding number of directors attended the various board meetings is shown in annual report. Particulars of the directorships/ memberships held by them in other Boards/ Committees are presented in a separate Annexure.
2. IDBI	(1) Information about Salary & Perquisites paid to CMD and DMD is given and Sitting Fees paid to other directors is not mentioned. (2) No brief Resume of Exec. and non-executive director is given. (3) Table regarding number of directors attended the various board meetings is shown along withDirectorship and Committee Membership of board members.

(Contd...)

3. SIDBI	(1) No information about Salary and Perquisites paid to Chairman and Managing Director is given and Sitting Fees paid to Other Directors is also not mentioned. (2) No brief Resume of Executive and non-executive director is given. (3) No Table regarding number of directors attended the various board meetings is shown and no information on Directorship and Committee Membership of board members is given. Total number of board meeting held is only given.
4. IFCI	(1) Information about Salary and Perquisites paid to CMD is given and Sitting Fees paid to other Directors is also mentioned. (2) No brief Resume of Executive and non-executive director is given. (3) Tables regarding the names of individual directors describing their category along with attendance particulars and Committee Membership of board members are given.
5. LICI	(1) Information about Salary and Perquisites paid to CMD is given and Sitting Fees paid to other Directors is also mentioned. (2) No brief resume of directors is given, (3) No table regarding director's attendance of meetings is given but information on directorship and committee membership of Board members is given.
6. HDFC	(1) Aggregate Salary and Perquisites paid to Executive Directors is given and Sitting fees paid to other Directors is mentioned. (2) Brief Resume of Executive and non-executive director is given. (3) Tables for Attendance of individual members are shown according to various committees and Directorship and Committee Membership of board members is also given.
7. PNB	(1) Information about salary and sitting fees of directors is given, (2) No brief Resume of Executive and non-executive director is given but profile of newly appointed Directors is given, (3) Tables for attendance of directors in the meeting is given.
8. BOB	(1) Information about salary and sitting fees of directors is given .(2) No brief Resume of Executive and non- executive director is given, only newly appointed directors profile is given, (3) Tables for Attendance of individual members are shown according to various committees and Directorship and Committee Membership of board members is also given.

(Contd...)

9. BOL	(1) Information about salary and sitting fees of directors is given, (2) Brief resume of newly appointed MD/ Chairman is given, (3) Tables for Attendance of individual members are shown according to various committees and board meeting and Directorship and Committee Membership of board members is also given.
10. UBI	(1) No information about salary and sitting fees of directors is given, (2) Brief resume of newly appointed director's are given, (3) Tables for Attendance of individual members are shown according to various committees and board meeting and Directorship & Committee Membership of board members is also given.
11. KMB	(1) Information about salary, perquisites and sitting fees of directors is given, (2) Brief resume of director's are given, (3) Tables for Attendance of individual members are shown according to various committees and board meeting and Directorship and Committee Membership of board members is also given.
12. NHB	(1) No information about salary and sitting fees paid to directors, (2) No brief resume of director's are given but profile of newly directors are given, (3) No information about attendance of individual members are shown according to various committees and board meeting and Directorship and Committee Membership of board members is also given.
13. NABARD	(1) No information about salary and sitting fees of directors is given, (2) Brief resume of newly appointed director's are given, (3) Tables for Attendance of individual members are shown according to various committees and board meeting and Directorship and Committee Membership of board members is also given.

Table 4.5 Organizational Committees

Name of Financial Institutions	*Organizational Committees*
1. SBI	The Central Board has constituted Eight Committees of Directors, namely, (1) Executive Committee, (2) Audit Committee, (3) Shareholders'/Investors' Grievance Committee, (4) Risk Management Committee of the Board and (5) Special Committee of Directors for Monitoring Large Value Frauds (Rs.1 Crore and above) Meetings of the Central Board and the Committees, (6) Customer Service Committee, (7) Technology Committee, (8) Remuneration Committee.
2. IDBI	The Board has in total eight committees, namely, (i) Executive Committee, (ii) Audit Committee, (iii) Shareholder's/Investor's Grievance Committee, (iv) Frauds Monitoring Committee, (v) Risk Management Committee, (vi) Customer Service Committee, (vii) Information Technology Committee and (viii) Remuneration Committee.
3. SIDBI	Seven major types of committees are framed by BOD's namely (1) Executive committee, (2) Audit Committee, (3) Central and Regional Credit committee, (4) Central and Regional settlement Committee, (5) Venture Capital Screening Committee (6) Asset Liability Management Committee and (7) Advisory Committees.
4. IFCI	Three committee are framed as per lines with Code of Corporate Governance by the BOD's of IFCI namely (1)Audit Committee, (2) Remuneration Committee and (3) Investors Grievance Committee.
5. LICI	As per Section 19 of Life Insurance Corporation Act, 1956, Executive Committee and Investment Committee are formed by the Board. Further one Building Advisory Committee has also been formed to guide LIC in Estates matters. Another committee named Central Management Committee is also constituted. Therefore only four committees are there and no Audit Committee is formed.

(Contd...)

6. HDF	Nine major types of committees are framed by BOD's viz., (i) Audit and Compliance Committee, (ii) Compensation Committee, (iii) Investor Grievance (Share) Committee, (iv) Risk Monitoring Committee, (v) Fraud Monitoring Committee, (vi) Credit Approval Committee, (vii) Premises Committee, (viii) Nomination Committee and (ix) Customer Service Committee.
7. PNB	There are sixteen committees in the bank viz., 1. Management Committee, 2. Audit Committee of Board, 3. Risk Management Committee, 4. Share Transfer Committee, 5. Shareholders' /Investors' Grievance Committee, 6. Customer Service Committee, 7. I.T. Committee 8. PA Committee, 9. Director's Promotion Committee, 10. Appellate Authority and Reviewing Authority, 11. Special Committee of Board to monitor and follow up fraud cases involving Rs. One Crore and above, 12. Committee of Directors to Review Vigilance and Non-Vigilance cases, 13. HRD Committee of Directors, 14. Remuneration Committee, 15. Nomination Committee 16. Steering Committee for Vision 2013.
8. BOB	Ten committees are constituted by the Board viz., (i) Management Committee of the Board, (ii) Audit Committee of Board (ACB), (iii) Shareholders'/ Investors' Grievances Committee, (iv) Share Transfer Committee, (v) Asset Liability Management and Risk Management Committee, (vi) Customer Service Committees, (vii) Remuneration Committee, (viii) Nomination Committee, (ix) Committee of Directors, (x) Committee on High Value Frauds.
9. BOI	Three committees are constituted by the Board namely, (i) Management Committee of the Board, (ii) Audit Committee of the Board, and (iii) Shareholders'/ Investors' Grievance Committee.
10. UBI	There are 8 committees in the bank viz., (i) Management Committee, (ii) Audit Committee (iii) Risk Management Committee, (iv) Special Committee of the Board for monitoring large value Frauds, (v) Customer Service Committee , (vi) High Power Committee, (vii) Remuneration Committee, and (viii) IT Sub- Committee.

(Contd...)

11. KMB	The Board has constituted 14 committees to deal with specific matters and delegated powers for different functional areas. (i) The Audit Committee, (ii) Shareholders'/Investor's Grievance Committee, (iii) ESOP/Compensation Committee, (iv) Share Transfer and Routine Transactions Committee (START), (v) Management Committee, (vi) Premises Committee, (vii) Asset Liability Committee (ALCO), (viii) Nomination Committee, (ix) Investment Committee, (x) Risk Management Committee, (xi) Information Technology Committee, (xii) First Tier Audit Committee, (xiii) Customer Services Committee, and (xiv) Committee on Frauds.
12. NHB	The Board has constituted two Committees, viz., (a) Executive Committee of Directors [EC] and (b) Audit Committee of the Board [ACB] to enable better and focused attention on the affairs of the Bank. In addition to above, the Board has constituted a Committee of Directors (C-BSOS) to review the Business Strategy and Organization Structure of the Bank. Therefore only three committees are there in the bank.
13. NABARD	The Board has constituted four Committees viz., (i) Executive Committee, (ii) Audit Committee, (iii) Sanctioning Committee, and (iv) Risk Management Committee

Table 4.6 Additional Information Disclosed in the Annual Report

Other Information	*SBI*	*IDBI*	*SIDBI*	*IFCI*	*LICI*	*HDFC*	*PNB*	*BOB*	*BOI*	*UBI*	*KMB*	*NHB*	*NABARD*
1. Separate Report on Corporate Governance	Y	Y	N	Y	N	Y	Y	Y	N	Y	Y	Y	N
2. Information of AGM of Shareholders Stakeholder information	Y	Y	N	Y	N	Y	Y	Y	Y	Y	Y	N	N
3. Market information Data	Y	Y	N	Y	N	Y	Y	Y	Y	Y	Y	N	N
4. Shareholding Pattern	Y	Y	Y	Y	N	Y	Y	Y	Y	Y	Y	N	N
5. Address for Correspondence	Y	Y	N	Y	N	Y	Y	N	N	Y	N	N	N
6. Details of Dematerialization	N	Y	N	Y	N	Y	Y	Y	Y	Y	N	N	N
7. Acknowledgement	N	Y	Y	Y	Y	Y	Y	Y	Y	Y	Y	N	Y
8 Details of Employee Stock Option	N	Y	N	Y	N	Y	N	N	N	N	Y	N	N
9. Review of Chairman of Various Committees	N	N	N	Y	N	Y	N	N	N	N	N	N	N

(Contd...)

10. Directors Report on Corporate Governance	Y	Y	N	Y	N	Y	Y	Y	Y	Y	Y	N	N
11. Auditors report on corporate governance	Y	Y	N	Y	N	Y	Y	Y	Y	Y	Y	N	N
12. Promotion of Official Language	Y	Y	Y	N	Y	N	Y	Y	Y	N	N	Y	Y
13. Disclosure under Basel Norms	BS II	N	N	N	N	BS II	BS II	BS II	BS II	BS III	BS II	N	N
14. Accounting Policies and Standards	Y	Y	Y	Y	Y	Y	Y	Y	Y	Y	Y	N	Y
15. Whistle Blower Policy	N	Y	N	N	N	Y	Y	Y	N	Y	Y	N	N
16. External credit rating (Domestic, Overseas and Rating/BCSBI)	N	Y (Both D & O)	N	N	N	Y (Both D & O)	Y (Both D & O)	Y (Both D, O & CG	Y (Both D, O & BCS BI	Y (Both D, O & BCS BI	N	N	N
17. Information about Director seeking appointment/ reappointment as directors	N	N	N	Y	N	N	N	N	N	Y	N	N	N
18. Nos of Board Meeting Held	10	8	-	4	4	6	3	8	6	4	10	-	-

(Contd...)

Other Information	*SBI*	*IDBI*	*SIDBI*	*IFCI*	*LICI*	*HDFC*	*PNB*	*BOB*	*BOI*	*UBI*	*KMB*	*NHB*	*NABARD*
19. Details of composition and functions of committees	Y	Y	N	Y	Y	Y	Y	Y	Y	Y	Y	N	Y
20 Multiple Board seats (Directors in other Cos Directors as members in other committees Directors as Chairperson in other committees)Max	21/ */9	13/ */*	-	8/6/ 2	13/* */*	13/* /*	*/1 3/8	9/7 /*	5/4 /3	8/6 /5	11/ 2/4	-	-
21. Related Party Disclosure AS -18	Y	Y	Y	Y	Y	Y	Y	Y	Y	Y	Y	Y	Y
TOTAL SCORE	15	14	05	17	07	19	18	17	15	18	15	04	05

ANNEXURE - I

I. CADBURY CODE OF BEST PRACTICES

The Cadbury Code of Best Practices had 19 recommendations. The recommendations are in the nature of guidelines relating to Board of Directors, Non-executive Directors, Executive Directors and those on Reporting and Control.

Relating to the Board of Directors

- The Board should meet regularly retain full and effective control over the company and monitor the executive management.
- There should be a clearly accepted division of responsibilities at the head of a company, which will ensure balance of power and authority, such that no individual has unfettered powers of decision. In companies where the Chairman is also the Chief Executive, it is essential that there should be a strong and independent element on the Board, with a recognized senior member.
- The Board should include non-executive Directors of sufficient caliber and number for their views to carry significant weight in the Board's decisions.
- The Board should have a formal schedule of matters specifically reserved to it for decisions to ensure that the direction and control of the company is firmly in its hands.
- There should be an agreed procedure for Directors in the furtherance of their duties to take independent professional advice if necessary, at the company's expense.
- All directors should have access to the advice and services of the Company Secretary, who is responsible to the Board for ensuring that Board procedures are followed and that applicable rules and regulations are complied with. Any question of the removal of Company Secretary should be a matter for the Board as a whole.

Relating to the Non-Executive Directors Recommendations Are:

- Non-executive Directors should bring an independent judgement to bear on issues of strategy, performance, resources, including key appointments, and standards of conduct.
- The majority should be independent of the management and free from any business or other relationship, which could materially interfere with the exercise of their independent judgement, apart from their fees and shareholding. Their fees should reflect the time, which they commit to the company.
- Non-executive Directors should be appointed for specified terms and reappointment should not be automatic.
- Non-executive Directors should be selected through a formal process and both, this process and their appointment, should be a matter for the Board as a whole.

Relating to the Executive Directors

- Director's service contracts should not exceed three years without shareholders' approval.
- There should be full and clear disclosure of their total emoluments and those of the Chairman and the highest-paid UK Directors, including pension contributions and stock options. Separate figures should be given for salary and performance-related elements and the basis on which performance is measured should be explained.
- Executive Directors' pay should be subject to the recommendations of a Remuneration Committee made up wholly or mainly of Non-executive Directors.

On Reporting and Controls

- It is the Board's duty to present a balanced and understandable assessment of the company's position.
- The Board should ensure that an objective and professional relationship is maintained with the Auditors.

- The Board should establish an Audit Committee of at least three Non-executive Directors with written terms of reference, which deal clearly with its authority and duties.
- The Directors should explain their responsibility for preparing the accounts next to a statement by the Auditors about their reporting responsibilities.
- The Directors should report on the effectiveness of the company's system of internal control.
- The Directors should report that the business is a going concern, with supporting assumptions or qualifications as necessary.

II. 'FIT AND PROPER' CRITERIA FOR DIRECTORS OF BANKS

In exercise of the powers conferred by Section 35A of the Banking Regulation Act, 1949 and on being satisfied that it is necessary and expedient in public interest so to do, the Reserve Bank of India (Circular DBOD.No.BC.104/ 08.139.001/2003-04 dated June 25, 2004) hereby directs, with immediate effect that:

(i) the banks in private sector should undertake a process of due diligence to determine the suitability of the person for appointment / continuing to hold appointment as a director on the Board, based upon qualification, expertise, track record, integrity and other fit and proper criteria. Banks should obtain necessary information and declaration from the proposed / existing directors for the purpose

(ii) The process of due diligence should be undertaken by the banks in private sector at the time of appointment/ renewal of appointment.

(iii) The boards of the banks in private sector should constitute Nomination Committees to scrutinize the declarations.

(iv) Based on the information provided in the signed declaration, Nomination Committees should decide on the acceptance and may make references, where considered necessary to the appropriate authority / persons, to ensure their compliance with the requirements indicated.

(v) Banks should obtain annually a simple declaration that the information already provided has not undergone change and where there is any change, requisite details are furnished by the directors forthwith.

(vi) The board of the bank must ensure in public interest that nominated/elected directors execute the deeds of covenants as recommended by Dr. Ganguly Group every year.

III. DR. GANGULY COMMITTEE

List of recommendations of the Consultative Group of Directors of banks and financial institutions which may be considered by banks for adoption and implementation.

A. Recommendations which may be implemented by all banks

(i) Responsibilities of the Board of Directors

(a) A strong corporate board, should fulfill the following four major roles viz. overseeing the risk profile of the bank, monitoring the integrity of its business and control mechanisms, ensuring the expert management and maximizing the interests of its stakeholders.

(b) The Board of Directors should ensure that responsibilities of directors are well defined and every director should be familiarized on the functioning of the bank before his induction, covering the following essential areas:

- delegation of powers to various authorities by the Board,
- strategic plan of the institution,
- organizational structure,
- financial and other controls and systems,
- Economic features of the market and competitive environment.

(ii) Role and Responsibility of Independent and Non-Executive Directors

(a) The independent/non-executive directors have a prominent role in inducting and sustaining a pro-active governance framework in banks.

(b) In order to familiarize the independent /non-executive directors with the environment of the bank, banks may circulate among the new directors a brief note on the profile of the bank, the sub-committees of the Board, their role, details on delegation of powers, the profiles of the top executives etc.

(c) It would be desirable for the banks to take an undertaking from each independent and non-executive director to the effect that he/she, has gone through the guidelines defining the role and responsibilities and enter into covenant to discharge his/her responsibilities to the best of their abilities, individually and collectively.

(iii) Training Facilities for Directors

(a) Need-based training programmes / seminars / workshops may be designed by banks to acquaint their directors with emerging developments/challenges facing the banking sector and participation in such programmes could make the directors more sensitive to their role.

(b) The Board should ensure that the directors are exposed to the latest managerial techniques, technological developments in banks, and financial markets, risk management systems etc. so as to discharge their duties to the best of their abilities.

(c) While RBI can offer certain training programmes/ seminars in this regard at its training establishments, large banks may conduct such programmes in their own training centers.

(iv) Submission of Routine Information to the Board

Reviews dealing with various performance areas may be put up to the Management Committee of the Board and only a summary on each of the reviews may be put up to the Board of Directors at periodic intervals. This will provide the Board more time to concentrate on more strategic issues such as risk profile, internal control systems, overall performance of the bank etc.

(v) Agenda and Minutes of the Board Meeting

(a) The draft minutes of the meeting should be forwarded to the, directors, preferably via the electronic media, within 48 hours of the meeting and ratification obtained from the directors within a definite time frame. The directors may be provided with necessary technology assistance towards this end.

(b) The Board should review the status of the action taken on points arising from the earlier meetings till action is completed to the satisfaction of the Board, and any pending item should be continued to be put up as part of the agenda items before the Board.

(vi) Committees of the Board

(a) Shareholders' Redressal Committee

As communicated to banks in our circular DBOD No.111/ 08.138.001/2001-02 dated June 4, 2002 on SEBI Committee on Corporate Governance, the banks which have issued shares/debentures to public may form a committee under the chairmanship of a non-executive director to look into the redressal of shareholders' complaints.

(b) Risk Management Committee

In pursuance of the Risk Management Guidelines issued by the Reserve Bank of India in October 1999, every banking organisation is required to set up Risk Management Committee. The formation and operationalisation of such committee should be speeded up and their role further strengthened.

(c) Supervisory Committee

The role and responsibilities of the Supervisory Committee as envisaged by the Group viz., monitoring of the exposures (both credit and investment) of the bank, review of the adequacy of the risk management process and upgradation thereof, internal control system, ensuring compliance with the statutory/regulatory framework etc., may be assigned to the Management Committee/Executive Committee of the Board.

(vii) Disclosure and Transparency

The following disclosures should be made by banks to the Board of Directors at regular intervals as may be prescribed by the Board in this regard.

- Progresses made in putting in place a progressive risk management system, and risk management policy and strategy followed by the bank.
- Exposures to related entities of the bank, viz. details of lending to/investment in subsidiaries, the asset classification of such lending/investment, etc.
- Conformity with corporate governance standards viz. in composition of various committees, their role and functions, periodicity of the meetings and compliance with coverage and review functions etc.

B. Recommendations Applicable only Public Sector Banks

(i) Information flow

In order to improve manner in which the proceedings are recorded and followed up in public sector banks, they may initiate measures to provide the following information to the board:

- A summary of key observations made by the directors, which should be submitted, in the next board meeting.
- A more detailed recording of the proceedings which will clearly bring out the observations, dissents, etc. by the individual directors which could be forwarded to them for their confirmation.

(ii) Company Secretary

The Company Secretary has important fiduciary and Company Law responsibilities. The Company Secretary is the nodal point for the Board to get feedback on the status of compliance by the organization in regard to provisions of the Company Law, listing agreements, SEBI regulations, shareholder grievances, etc. In view of the important role performed by the Company Secretary vis-à-vis the functioning of the Boards of the banks, as also in the context of some of the public sector banks having made public issue it may be necessary to have Company Secretary for these banks also. Banks should therefore consider appointing qualified Company Secretary as the Secretary to-the Board and have a Compliance Officer (reporting to the Secretary) for ensuring compliance with various regulatory / accounting requirements.

C. Recommendations Applicable to Private Sector banks

(i) Eligibility criteria and 'fit and proper' norms for nomination of directors.

(a) The Board of Directors of the banks while nominating / co-opting directors should be guided by certain broad 'fit and proper' norms for directors, viz. formal qualification, experience, track record, integrity etc. For assessing integrity and suitability features like criminal records, financial position, civil actions initiated to pursue personal debts, refusal of admission to or expulsion from professional bodies, sanctions applied by regulators or similar bodies, previous questionable business practices etc. should be considered. The Board of Directors may, therefore, evolve appropriate systems for ensuring 'fit and proper' norms for directors, which may include calling for information by way of self-declaration, verification reports from market, etc.

(b) The following criteria, which is in vogue in respect of nomination to the boards of public sector banks, may also be followed for nominating independent/non-executive directors on private sector banks:

- The candidate should normally be a graduate (which can be relaxed while selecting directors for the categories of farmers, depositors, artisans, etc.)
- He/she should be between 35 and 65 years of age.
- He/she should not be a Member of Parliament / Member of Legislative Assembly/Member of Legislative Council.

(ii) Commonality of Directors of Banks and Non-Banking Finance Companies (NBFC)

In case, a director on the board of an NBFC is to be considered for appointment as director on the board of the bank, the following conditions must be followed:

- He/she is not the owner of the NBFC, [i.e., share holdings (single or jointly with relatives, associates, etc.) should not exceed 50 per cent.
- He/she is not related to the promoter of the NBFC.
- He/she is not a full-time employee in the NBFC.
- The concerned NBFC is not a borrower of the bank.

(iii) Composition of the Board.

In the context of banking becoming more complex and competitive, the composition of the Board should be commensurate with the business needs of the banks. There is an urgent need for making the Boards of banks more contemporarily professional by inducting technical and specially qualified personnel. Efforts should be aimed at bringing about a blend of 'historical skills' set, i.e., regulation based representation of sectors like agriculture, SSI, cooperation etc. and the 'new skills' set, i.e., need based representation of skills such as, marketing, technology and systems, risk management, strategic planning, treasury operations, credit recovery etc. The above suggestions may be kept in view while electing/co-opting directors to their boards.

IV. SUMMARY OF THE IMPORTANT RECOMMENDATIONS OF THE SEBI'S COMMITTEE ON CORPORATE GOVERNANCE

The Securities and Exchange Board of India (SEBI) had constituted a Committee on Corporate Governance and circulated the recommendations to all stock exchanges for implementation by listed entities as part of the listing agreement vide SEBI's circular SMDRP/Policy/CIR-10/2000 dated February 21, 2000. Full text of recommendations of the Committee which form part of the above circular can be had by access to SEBI's website:www.sebi.gov.in/circulars/2000. A summary of the important recommendations of the SEBI's Committee as applicable to banks is furnished here under:

1.1. All pecuniary relationship or transactions of the non-executive directors should be disclosed in the annual report.

1.2. The Committee is of the view that non-executive directors help bring an independent judgment to bear on board's deliberations, especially on issues of strategy, performance, management of conflicts and standards of conduct. The Committee therefore lays emphasis on the calibre of the non-executive directors, especially of the independent directors.

1.3. The Committee is of the view that it is important that an adequate compensation package be given to the non-executive independent directors so that these positions become sufficiently financially attractive to attract talent and that the non-executive directors are sufficiently compensated for undertaking this work.

1.4. The Committee recommends that the board of a company have an optimum combination of executive and non-executive directors with not less than fifty per cent of the board comprising the non-executive directors. The number of independent directors depends on the nature of the chairman of the board. In case a company has a non-executive chairman, at least half of board should be independent (Mandatory recommendation).

2.1 The Committee recommends that when a nominee of the institutions is appointed as a director of the company, he should have the same responsibility, be subject to the same discipline and be accountable to the shareholders in the same manner as any other director of the company. In particular, if he reports to any department of the institutions on the affairs of the company, the institution should ensure that there exist Chinese walls between such department and other department which may be dealing in the shares of the company in the stock market.

3.1 The Committee recommends that a non-executive Chairman should be entitled to maintain a Chairman's office at the company's expense and also allowed reimbursement of expenses incurred in performance of his duties. This will enable him to discharge the responsibilities effectively.

The Committee recommends that a qualified and independent audit committee should be set up by the board of a company (Mandatory recommendation).

The Committee recommends that-

- the audit committee should have a minimum of three members, all being non-executive directors, with the majority being independent and with at least one director having financial and accounting knowledge;
- the chairman of the committee should be an independent director;
- the chairman should be present at the Annual General Meeting to answer shareholder's queries;
- The audit committee should invite such of the executives, as it considers appropriate (and particularly the head of the finance function) to be present at the meetings of the Committee but on occasions it may also meet without the presence of any executives of the company. The finance director and head of internal audit and when required, a representative of the external auditor should be present as invitees for the meetings of the audit committee;
- The Company Secretary should act as the secretary to the committee.

4.1 The Committee recommends that the audit committee should meet at least thrice a year. One meeting must be held before finalisation of annual accounts and one necessarily every six months (Mandatory recommendation).

4.2 The quorum should be either two members or one-third of the members of the audit committee, whichever is higher and there should be a minimum of two independent directors (Mandatory recommendation).

4.3 Being a committee of the board, the audit committee derives its powers from the authorization of the board. The Committee recommends that such powers should include powers:

1. to investigate any activity within its terms of reference.
2. to seek information from any employee.
3. to obtain outside legal or other professional advice.
4. to secure attendance of outsiders with relevant expertise, if it considers necessary.

- Discussion with external auditors, before the audit commences, of the nature and scope of audit. Also post-audit discussion to ascertain any area of concern.
- Reviewing the company's financial and risk management policies.
- Looking into the reasons for substantial defaults in the payments to the depositors, debenture holders, shareholders (in case of non-payment of declare dividends) and creditors.

This is a Mandatory Recommendation.

4.6 As the audit committee acts as the bridge between the board, the statutory auditors and internal auditors, the Committee recommends that its role should include the following:

- Oversight of the company's financial reporting process and the disclosure of its financial information to ensure that the financial statement is correct, sufficient and credible.

- Recommending the appointment and removal of the external auditor, fixation of audit fee and also approval for payment for any other service.
- Reviewing with management the annual financial statements before submission to the board, focusing primarily on:
  - o Any changes in accounting policies and practices.
  - o Major accounting entries based on exercise of judgement by management.
  - o Qualifications in draft audit report.
  - o Significant adjustment arising out of audit.
  - o The going concern of assumption.
  - o Compliance with accounting standards.
  - o Compliance with stock exchange and legal requirement concerning financial institutions.
  - o Any related party transactions i.e. transactions of the company of material nature, with promoters or the management, their subsidiaries or relatives, etc., that may have potential conflict with the interests of company the at large.
- Reviewing with the management, external and internal auditors, the adequacy of internal control systems.
- Reviewing the adequacy of the internal audit function, including the structure of the internal audit department, staffing and seniority of the official heading the department, reporting structure, coverage and frequency of internal audit.
- Discussion with the internal auditors of any significant findings and follow-up thereon.
- Reviewing the findings of any internal investigations by the internal auditors into matters where there is suspected fraud or irregularity or a failure of internal control systems of a material nature and reporting the matter to the board.

5.1 The Committee recommends that the board should set up a remuneration committee to determine on their behalf and on behalf of the shareholders with agreed terms of reference, the company's policy on specific remuneration packages for executive directors including pension rights and any compensation payment.

6.1 The Committee therefore recommends that board meetings should be held at least four times in a year, with a maximum time gap of four months between any two meetings. The minimum information should be available to the board (Mandatory recommendation).

6.2 The committee recommends that a director should not be a member in more than 10 committees or act as Chairman of more than five committees across all companies in which he is a director. Furthermore, it is a mandatory annual requirement for every director to inform the company about the committee positions he occupies in other companies and notify changes as and when they take place (Mandatory recommendation).

7.1 The recommendations contained in this section pertain to accounting standards on consolidation, segment reporting, disclosure and treatment of related party transactions and deferred taxation. The Committee recommended that the Institute of Chartered Accountants of India issue accounting standards on these areas expeditiously.

8.1 As a part of the disclosure related to Management, the Committee recommends that as part of the directors' report or as an addition thereto, a Management Discussion and Analysis report should form part of the annual report to the shareholders (Mandatory recommendation).

8.2 The committee recommends that disclosures be made by management to the, board relating to all material financial and commercial transactions, where they have personal interest, that may have a potential conflict with the interest of the company at large (for e.g. dealing in company shares, commercial dealings with bodies which have shareholding of management and their relatives etc. (Mandatory recommendation).

9.1 The Committee recommends that in case of the appointment of a new director or re-appointment of a director the shareholders must be provided with the following information:

- A brief resume of the director;
- Nature of his expertise in specific financial areas; and
- Names of the companies in which the person also holds the directorship and the membership of Committees of the board.

9.2 The Committee recommends that information like quarterly results, presentation made by companies to analysts may be put on company's website 6r may be sent in such a form so as to enable the stock exchange on which the company is listed to put it on its own website (Mandatory recommendation).

9.3 The Committee recommends that the half-yearly declaration of financial performance including summary of the significant events in last six months, should be sent to each household of shareholders.

9.4 The Committee recommends that a board committee under the chairmanship of a non-executive director should be formed to specifically look into the redressing of shareholder complaints like transfer of shares, non-receipt of balance sheet, non-receipt of declared dividends etc. The Committee believes that the formation of such a committee will help focus the attention of the company on shareholders' grievances and sensitize the management to redressal of their grievances (Mandatory recommendation).

9.5 The Committee further recommends that to expedite the process of share transfers the board of the company should delegate the power of share transfer to an officer, or a committee or to the registrar and share transfer agents. The delegated authority should attend to share transfer formalities at least once in a fortnight (Mandatory recommendation).

10 The Committee recommends that there should be a separate section on Corporate Governance in the annual reports of companies, with a detailed compliance report on Corporate Governance. Non-compliance of any mandatory recommendation with reasons thereof and the extent to which the non-mandatory recommendations have been adopted should be specifically highlighted. This will enable the shareholders and the securities market to assess for themselves the standards of corporate governance followed by a company. (Mandatory recommendation).

References

Annual Reports- 2009-10

- IDBI—Industrial Development Bank of India
- SIDBI—Small Industries Development Bank of India
- IFCI—Industrial Financial Corporation of India
- NABARD— National Bank for Agriculture and Rural Development
- PNB— Punjab National Bank
- UBI—United Bank of India
- BOB— Bank of Baroda
- BOI—Bank of India
- LICI—Life Insurance Corporation of India
- KMB—Kotak Mahindra Bank
- NHB—National Housing Bank
- HDFC- Housing Development Finance Corporation

Bibliographic

1. Report of the Consultative Group of Directors of Banks and Financial Institutions, April 2004.
2. Report of the Recommendations of the Advisory Groups constituted by the Standards Committee on International Financial Standards & Codes: Report on the Progress and Agenda Ahead, Dec. 2002.
3. The Corporate Governance of Banks: A Concise Discussion of Concepts and Evidences", Discussion Paper No. 3, World Bank, 2003.

4. Government Ownership of Banks", Discussion Paper No. 1890, Harvard Institute of Economic Research, Harvard University, February 2002.

5. 5. Sir Adrian Cadbury, "Developments in Corporate Governance", The Company Secretary, The Institute of Chartered Secretary of India, New Delhi, May 97, p. 497.

6. Bhattacharya, S., Boot, A.W.A. and Thakor, A.V., "The Economics of Bank Regulation", *Journal of Money, Credit and Banking,* Vol. 30, 1998, 745-770.

7. Cadbury Committee (1992), Report of the Committee on the Financial Aspects of Corporate Governance, Gee and Co. London.

8. Chakrabarti, A; W. Megginson and P. Yadav, Corporate Governance in India, Working pp. No. 08-02, Centre for Financial Research.

9. CII (1998), Desirable Corporate Governance—A Code, http://www.CII.com

10. Confederation of Indian Industry (CII): Desirable Corporate Governance—A Code, Final Report: India, April 1998.

11. Confederation of Indian Industry, Report of the CII Task, Force on Corporate Governance, Chaired by Mr. Naresh Chandra, November 2009.

12. Das, A. and S. Ghosh, 2004. Corporate Governance in Banking System: An Empirical Investigation, *Economic and Political Weekly,* March 20, 2004, pp. 1263-1266.

13. Dimple Grover, Amulya Khurana, Ravi Shankar, 'The Regulatory Norms of Corporate Governance in India'.

14. Dr. A. P. Pati, Dose Corporate Governance Matter in Indian Banking? Policy Implications on the Performance.

15. Exposure Draft on Corporate Governance—May 2009.doc

16. Gopinath, Shyamala., "Corporate Governance towards Best Practices", *RBI*, Dec. 2004, 1105-1109.

17. Goswami, Omkar, 2002, "Corporate Governance in India," Taking Action Against Corruption in Asia and the Pacific (Manila: Asian Development Bank), Chapter 9.

18. Jalan, Bimal, Inaugural Address at NIBM Annual Day (6th January) on the theme of Corporate a Governance in Banks and Financial Institutions, NIBM, 2004.

19. Jayanth Rama Varma, Corporate Governance in India: Disciplining the Dominant Shareholder, IIMB Management Review available at http://www.iimb.ernet.in/review.

20. Joshi, Prof. Amitabh, *Corporate Governance in Indian Public Financial Institutions.*

21. Joshi, V. (2004) Corporate Governance: *The Indian Scenario,* Foundation Books.

22. Kamesam, Vepa, "Cooperative Banks in India: Strengthening Through Corporate Governance", *RBI Bulletin*, Vol. LVI, (8), August 2002, 551-557.

23. Kumar, Sunil and Verma, Satish, "Technical Efficiency, Benchmarks and Targets: A Case Study of Indian Public Sector Banks", *Prajnan*, Vol. XXXI, (4), Jan-Mar, 2003, 275-300.

24. La Porta, R., Lopez-de-Silanes, F. and Shleifer, A., "Corporate Ownership around the World", *Journal of Finance,* Vol. 54, 1999, 471-517.

25. Leeladhar, V., "Corporate Governance in Banks", *RBI*, Dec. 2004, 1101-1104.

26. London Stock Exchange (LSE): Committee on Corporate Governance, Hampel: The Combined Code, London, June 1998.

27. Madhu Sehgal and Annu Sarin (2003), *Corporate Governance and Financial Reporting in Indian Public Sector Banks,* New Delhi, Chartered Secretary, January 2003, pp No. 17-19

28. New York Stock Exchange and National Association of Corporate Directors (NACD): Report of the NACD Blue Ribbon Commission on Improving the Effectiveness of Corporate Audit Committees, New York, December 1998.

29. Organisation for Economic Co-operation and Development (OECD): Principles of Corporate Governance, Paris, May 1999.

30. Rajesh Chakrabarti, *Corporate Governance in India–Evolution and Challenges.*

31. Ram Mohan, T.T., "Deregulation and Performance of Public Sector Banks", *EPW*, Feb. 2, Vol. XXXVII, (5), 2002, 393-397.

32. RBI, Report of the Advisory Group on Corporate Governance, March, 2001.

33. Reddy, Y. V., 2002. Public sector banks and the governance challenge - the Indian experience, *BIS Review* 25/2002, Bank for International Settlements, Basle.

34. Reports on Corporate Governance, (2004), *Economica India Info Services,* Academic Foundation.

35. Sameet Gambhir (2003), *Governance Audit: A Checklist*, New Delhi, Chartered Secretary, January 2003, pp. No. 20-23.

36. Sarkar, J. and S. Sarkar (2000), Large Shareholder Activism in Corporate Governance in Developing Countries: Evidence from India, *International Review of Finance*, 1, 161-194.

37. SEBI (1999) "Draft Report of the Kumar Manglam Birla Committee on Corporate Governance", http://www.SEBI.org

38. S.K. Chakraborty (2002), "Corporate Governance for India – some pointers, Productivity" Vol. 40 No. 4, January- March 2002, pp No. 507-510.

39. T. P. Ghosh, Corporate Governance Model and Disclosure (2002), Productivity, Vol. 40 No. 4, January- March 2002, pp. No. 519-529.

40. Bies, S.S., "Bank Performance and Corporate Governance", *BIS Review,* No. 55, Bank for International Settlement, Basel, 2002.

41. CG_Voluntary_Guidelines_2009

Web Links References

1. http://www.sebi.gov.in/—Securities and Exchange Board of India
2. http://www.bseindia.com/—Bombay Stock Exchange Limited
3. http://www.nfcgindia.org/library_int.htm—National Foundation for Corporate Governance
4. http://www.ita.doc.gov/goodgovernance/—International Trade Administration
5. http://www.oecd.org/—Organisation for Economic Co-operation and Development
6. http://www.corpgov.net/—Corporate governance networ

Notes

1. Chakrabarti, A.W. Megginson And P. Yadav, "Corporate Governance in India" Working Paper No. 08-02, Centre for Financial Research.
2. See Rafael La Porta, Florencio Lopez-de-Silanes, Andrei Shleifer and Rob Vishny in their 1998, "Law and Finance" study, *Journal of Political Economy*, 106, pp 1113-1150.
3. See World Bank, 2008, *'Doing Business 2008'* World Bank and Oxford University Press, Washington, DC.
4. Suchismita Bose, 2005, "Securities Markets Regulation: Lessons from US and Indian Experience" , *Money and Finance,* Jan-June, pp 83-124.
5. http://www.amazon.com
6. http://www.iccwbo.org/CorpGov/whycorpgov.asp

7. http://www.asx.com.au/about/pdf/ASXRecommendations.pdf

8. Dr. A. P. Pati, "Does Corporate Governance Matter In Indian Banking? Policy Implications on the Performance".

9. Rajesh Chakrabarti, *Corporate Governance in India–Evolution and Challenges*

10. RBI/2009-10/17 DNBS (PD) CC No. 156/03.10.001/2009-10 July 1, 2009.

5

Non-Banking Financial Companies
Tragedy of Economic History of Modern India

Dr. K. S. Vataliya
Mr. H. D. Vyas

ABSTRACT

As per that financial sector was also deregulated to such extent for private Indian and foreign companies. Due to this many national and Multinational companies activated their activities in the area of Banking and Non-Banking financial services too. Moreover at the beginnings, LPG have attracted many newcomers in financial market. So jungle law of survival is prevalent in Indian financial market at present.

The objective of this paper is to study the Non-Banking Financial Companies of India in respect to their performance in the market. In India, the atmosphere is like law of seas where big fish swallows smaller, as per that huge and giant NBFC Companies or foreign companies are swallowing smaller NBFCs.

In past, large numbers of banking companies and financial institutions dreamed to expand their activities all over the world, but now only 10-12 players aim to expand their activities at world level.

The situations like the last stage of world war II in the field of financial services are prevailing in India. Infact few financial Companies or banks are expanding their activities with such ambitions. Many banks and financial institutions want to work in particular market with specific product instead of expanding their activities around the world.

The company who wants to go abroad has to consider local culture of the concerned country. We learnt a lesson in India after experience of huge losses. Even though having high means, companies did not use specialized skills and knowledge in a specific field. A large numbers. of Indian NBFCs is just like a tragedy of economic history of modern India.

Introduction

Many countries tested fruits of Liberalisation, Privatisation and Globalisation (LPG) and people of these countries are also getting their share according to contribution. Some countries have experienced adverse results of the same. And because of these results, economic existence of those countries has become endangered.

Since 1991 Indian Authorities opened the doors for LPG. As a part of this LPG process, many relaxations were declared in numerous areas of economy and production. As per that financial sector was also deregulated to such extent for private Indian and foreign companies. Due to this many national and Multinational companies activated their activities in the area of Banking and Non-Banking financial services too.

Currently Indian economy is passing through the situation of liquidity. Moreover at the beginnings, LPG have attracted many newcomers in financial market. They also began their activities in many areas of financial sector. But inefficiency of some of them put their existence in dangerous situation. Which affected their investor's economics too (Nemivant, 1999). So jungle law of survival is prevalent in Indian financial market at present.

We aspire to study the above in this paper. The objective of this paper is to study the Non-Banking Financial Companies of India in respect to their performance in the market. Therefore this paper is divided as (i) To study current position of Non-Banking Financial Companies (NBFCs) under Highlights, (ii) Present scenario, (iii) Survival of fittest, (iv) Lessons from experience and (v) Conclusion.

Highlights

1. Many companies, which are providing financial services to private sectors, have disappeared or they have been at last stage of end.
2. There is great disappointment and atmosphere of mistrust in this field. And the investors have lost crores of rupees.
3. In India, the atmosphere is like law of seas where big fish swallows smaller, as per that huge and giant NBFC Companies or foreign companies are swallowing smaller NBFCs.
4. In past, large numbers of banking companies and financial institutions dreamed to expand their activities all over the world, but now only 10-12 players aim to expand their activities at world level.
5. Compared to India, large and Multinational NBFCs in Britain, Germany, France and Japan feel wisdom to work in specific product and in particular field geographical area.
6. In India NBFCs are providing only financial services particularly lending activity. A very few NBFCs use skills or specific knowledge in the fields.

Present Scenario

The situations like the last stage of world war II in the field of financial services are prevailing in India. Five years, before all Industrial Houses were eager to tap in this field and so many companies were incorporated in financial services. They created euphoria in Indian capital market and as a result they issued their shares with high premium in the open market, and Indian investors were also ready to get the share at very high price without considering any norms of logical investments. During this period, number of companies has offered their issues in the market to gain investors' sentiment and collect millions of rupees from public. Public has lost crores of rupees due to failure of familiar and unfamiliar financial companies during last 5 to 7 years in our city. Numbers of companies have disappeared and remaining is at the last stage of TB (Rangarajan, 1996). A very few companies have survived, Industry scene is like a battlefield, where numbers of dead bodies are lying, others are handicapped and a very few soldiers are saved. This is the present seen of NBFCs of private sector.

As per experts' opinion such situation is due to keen competition in some fields. Norms for securities are neglected or not considered due to eagerness for enhancing business and overall bad conditions of the industry. Last layer of faith of investor is shacked by recent issue of CRB. As a result, possibilities of gaining money from public on competitive base are decreased and reached at last stage. In such a situation, it is difficult for Indian companies to start in market against more aggressive Banking companies, Government and Semi Government financial institution specifically huge foreign financing companies.

Survival of Fittest

Karl Marks says in his book Dascapital that if capitalisation is to be spread freely in the world, and restriction should not have been forced on it anywhere in the world, then 50 to 100 companies will be established their economic power in near future all over the world. Today when geographical boundary and artificial walls are going to break and consequent economic transactions are also going to be more free, then it is seemed that world is going to the path of forecasting of Karl Marks.

GE Capital, Morgan Stanley and Goodman Soch are going to cover Indian market strongly. In the initial stage, these international companies fail in the Indian market but it is clear they will be succeed in long run as their basis are strong and huge for setting up the high losses. As "big fishes are swallowind smaller fish" G.E. Capital has swallowed 1 or 2 Indian companies, ICICI swallowed ITC classic finance and now it is ready to absorb Anagram Finance via merger. Now other many Indian financial companies are in line to be a food of such giant companies. Now the days are not far away that financial service sector will remain for big players. Smaller companies are going to be disappeared (Shankaran, 2000). City Bank, A.B.N. Amro and United Bank of Switzerland are gradually increasing their presence at world level. Even though they learned through experience that it is not wise to offer each product to each market in every country.

As per Spokesman of Mackenzie and Company of New York, "Before some decades, there were about 50 countries in battles to lead the world in the field, which gradually decreased and reached at the No. of 20 companies and at present only 10-12 companies are in line.

In fact few financial companies or banks are expanding their activities with such ambitions. Many banks and financial institutions want to work in particular market with specific product instead of expanding their activities around the world.

Lessons from Experience

The policy document made it clear that as many as 37212 applications were received for registration as NBFCs. Of late even reputed NBFCs which are doing good business for the past many decades are also failing in doing the business, thereby causing a huge loss for small investors. The regulatory norms for formation of a self-regulatory organisation of NBFCs, disclosure norms and guidelines for risk management should be formed at the earliest. As, suggested by the Task Force headed by the Special Secretary (Banking) Shri C. M. Vasudev (Jain, 2000: 12).

Such multinational NBFCs have to pass through many kinds of experience, (good and bad) and change their future strategy. It is universally going to accept that the true power of the company is its product on which the construction is most important. The company who wants to go abroad has to consider local culture of concerned country. According to Prof. Ghoreli, of International Business School of losan, the company who wants to expand their activities have considered enough about its financial strength and skills, technology, strategy etc. but they are failed due to avoiding cope with local culture. [Such types of companies have to create belongings in the company by employing more and more internal experienced man from various countries.] There are about 9000 high level manager in City Bank are non-American and in its branches, out of them several are famous in their activities in the country.

At last, it is important that you develop your name as brand name around the globe, and then success will be in your hand.

Conclusion

Thus, particularly in India and around the world, there is quite disorder in the capital and money market. We learnt a lesson in India after experience of huge losses. In the last decade, leasing and financial companies which grew like a hot string in India research work has been done except lending the money neglecting security aspect (Tarapore, 2000). Our forefathers were also lending money and today we get money under the "English" words, collecting money from public, it is not new and it will not change the universal principles and rules. Even though having high means, companies did not use specialised skills and knowledge in a specific field. They did not contribute anything except huge expenses. A large number of Indian NBFCs is just like a tragedy of economic history of modern India. Because, some of the NBFCs becoming poisonous to the basic financial system itself (Jain, 2000: 13).

References

1. Jain, (Dr.) Jayanti Lal (2000), "Mid-Term Review of Monetary And Credit Policy", *IBA Bulletin,* XXII (10): 9-13.

2. Nemivant Tanuja (1999), "Software IPOs Going the NBFCs way", *Chartered Financial Analyst*, V (II): -.

3. Rangarajan, C. (1996), "The Role of Non-Banking Financial Companies in Financial Sector Development" in *'Banking and Financial Sector Reforms in India'*, ed. by: Raj Kapila and Uma Kapila, Academic Foundation Publication, New Delhi (1998): pp. 34-39.

4. Shankaran, Sanjiv (2000), "NBFCs: Banking on New Areas?" *ICFAI READER*, II (10): 31-39.5. Tarapore (2000), "Soul Searching on NBFCs", *ICFAI READER*, II (9): 39-40.

6

Prudential Way of Tapping Global Opportunities by Indian Companies

Mr. Giridhari Mohanta
Dr. Snehalkumar H Mistry

ABSTRACT

With the growth of the Indian economy at an average rate of 8.8 per cent every year, it may just prove to be an additional reason which triggers the growth in overseas investments. The data provided by the Reserve Bank of India for the year 2006 for the total value of Indian direct investments abroad was $ 9.7 billion. The latest World Bank report pegs India as the tenth largest economy in the world and the Goldman Sachs reports that India's GDP will top $1 trillion by 2011, treble by 2025 and be $27 trillion by 2025, taking its economy to third place after the US and China.

Introduction

The Indian M&A (mergers and acquisitions) boom witnessed in 2006 left many wondering whether there would be a slowdown in 2007 but the results of the first half proved them wrong. India's growth story continues to attract overseas investors and has also paved the way for Indian corporates to execute global strategies by acquiring companies both within and outside India not only to remain competitive but also to achieve scale.

The trend began haltingly a few years ago. In 2000, Tata Tea took over a global company twice its size, Tetley Tea, the second biggest tea company in the world. This was followed by Essel Packaging, owned by Subhash Chandra, took over Propack of Switzerland to form Essel Propack. The merger created the biggest producer in the world of laminated tubes, and an Indian MNC became global number one. But these takeovers remained exceptional events till 2003. Only in that year did the pace of Indian takeovers accelerate so much as to constitute a new trend. More than 40 foreign companies were taken over by Indians in 2003. Among the Indian companies on a takeover spree were Tata Motors, Ranbaxy, Wockhardt, Hindalco, etc. The trend of acquiring foreign companies was not limited to large size companies. Many middle-sized companies have also become a part of this new trend. Sundaram Fasteners has acquired Dana Spicer Europe, the British arm of a global multinational. Amtek Auto, another auto ancillary has acquired the GWK group in the UK, which is twice its size are some of the few middle sized companies which have joined the bandwagon. The trend continued with Indian companies shelling out $1.7 billion in the first eight months of 2005 for acquiring overseas companies. The biggest of the takeovers till date being the Tata Steel's $12.1 billion deal for Corus, the British steel company.

Factors behind the Growth of Indian Corporate on Global Front

The increased number in overseas acquisitions by Indian companies is attributable to the growing realization that the future growth of Indian companies will be influenced by the share that they can garner in the world market. This is not only by producing in the country and exporting, but also by acquiring overseas assets, including intangibles like brands and goodwill, to establish overseas presence and to upgrade their competitive strength in the overseas markets, which has resulted in cross-border acquisitions. The policy regime in respect of outward capital flows has also evolved in spirit with the above trend. In line with the calibrated approach to capital account, greater freedom is now available to companies to make remittances overseas for their overseas expansion. This is reflected in the increasing global operations of Indian companies in search of global synergies and domain knowledge. Phased liberalization in the policy of overseas investments has enabled Indian firms to establish presence in overseas markets on an unprecedented scale redefining the global outreach of Indian entities.

Liberalization of Overseas Investment Policy

The liberalization of investment policies has made large outward remittances for overseas acquisitions possible. Such policies have in particular expanded after the introduction of the Foreign Exchange Management Act, in June 2000. In March 2003, the Automatic Route was significantly liberalized to enable Indian parties to fund to the extent of 100 per cent of their net worth, which limit was later enhanced to 200 per cent. As per a recent study of Federation of Indian Chambers of Commerce and Industry (FICCI), while India Inc's international acquisitions were rising gradually till 2004, the liberalization in the policy regime for outward investment in 2005, which allowed Indian firms to invest in entities abroad up to 200 per cent of their net worth in a year, triggered a sharp rise in cross-border acquisitions with the number of acquisitions rising from 46 in 2004 to a whopping 130 in 2005.

During 2007-08 (April-December), 1,595 proposals were approved for investments abroad in JVs and WOSs by the Reserve Bank of India, which were higher by 25.8 per cent than approval during the corresponding period of the previous year. All these factors have provided the necessary thrust for the increase in the overseas investments and acquisitions.

Legal Framework

Indian companies wanting to acquire companies abroad have to comply with various aspects of the Companies Act of

1956, the Foreign Exchange Management Act of 1999, the Securities Exchange Board of India Act of 1992, and the various regulations imposed by the Reserve Bank of India. Also, the Take Over regulations applicable to the target company would need to be adhered to.

The Indian companies may invest overseas either through the automatic route or with the approval of the RBI. The present legal framework provides for investment overseas by Indian companies up to 200 per cent of their net worth as per the last audited balance sheet, in any bona fide business activity are permitted by Authorized Dealers (AD). Also no prior approval of RBI is required for opening offices abroad. For initial expenses, AD banks have been permitted to allow remittance up to 15 per cent of the average annual sales/income or turnover during last two financial years or up to 25 per cent of the net worth, whichever is higher.

For recurring expenses, remittance up to 10 per cent of the average annual sales/income or turnover during last two financial years is allowed. Within these limits, ADs can allow remittance by a company even to acquire immovable property outside India for its business and for residential purpose of its staff. The Indian investors would also have to file forms ODG/ODI depending on their method of investment in an overseas firm. The detailed guidelines have been provided under Notification FEMA 120/RB-2004 dated July 7, 2004, which is amended time to time.

Funding

Overseas acquisitions are being funded through a variety of sources such as drawal foreign exchange in India, capitalization of exports, balances held in Exchange Earner's Foreign Currency accounts (EEFC), share swaps through ADR/GDR, External Commercial Borrowings/Foreign Currency Convertible Bonds, ADRs/GDRs, etc.

A substantial portion of investments takes place through special purpose vehicles (SPVs) set up for the purpose abroad. Existing Wholly Owned Subsidiaries (WOS) / Joint Venture

(JV) or the SPVs are being used to fund acquisitions through Leveraged buy-out (LBO) route. In fact the Tata–Corus deal was made possible by the scheme of leveraged buy-out.

The major investment destinations appear to be the US and European markets. Tax havens like Mauritius and Cayman Islands also feature significantly in the Indian acquisitions or setting up of new WOS/JVs. In recent times, sustained growth in corporate earnings has boosted the profitability and strengthened the balance sheets of Indian companies. This has, in turn, strengthened their credit ratings and ability to raise funds overseas.

Unlike most international M&A transactions that typically feature stock swaps in the financing arithmetic, Indian acquirers have for the most part paid cash for their targets, helped by a combination of internal resources and borrowings. Share swaps have not yet emerged as a favoured payment option in India, except in a couple of large transactions in the software industry.

Finance by Indian Banks

In view of the expertise in certain areas developed by Indian corporates over the years and the importance attached to leveraging of such expertise for enhancing the international presence of Indian corporate, with effect from June 7, 2005, banks have been allowed to extend financial assistance to Indian companies for acquisition of equity in overseas joint ventures/wholly owned subsidiaries or in other overseas companies, new or existing, as strategic investment, in terms of a Board approved policy, duly incorporated in the loan policy of the bank. Such policy should include overall limit on such financing, terms and conditions of eligibility of borrowers, security, margin, etc. While the Board may frame its own guidelines and safeguards for such lending, such acquisition(s) should be beneficial to the company and the country. The finance would be subject to compliance with the statutory requirements under Section 19(2) of the Banking Regulation Act, 1949.

In April 2003 banks were permitted to extend credit/non-credit facilities to Indian Joint Ventures (JVs) (where the holding by the Indian company is more than 51%) / Wholly Owned Subsidiaries (WOS) abroad up to the extent of 10 per cent of their unimpaired capital funds subject to certain terms and conditions. On November 6, 2006, in order to facilitate the expansion of Indian corporate's business abroad, it was decided to enhance the prudential limit on credit and non-credit facilities extended by banks to Indian Joint Ventures (where the holding by the Indian company is more than 51%) /Wholly Owned Subsidiaries abroad from the existing limit of 10 per cent to 20 per cent of their unimpaired capital funds.

Modes for Tapping the Global Opportunities Merger

It is the mode in which two companies are merging their assets as well as liabilities, and operate as joint or single entity. In Merger activity, normally corporates involved are seeking the synergy effect or try to create synergy by complementing each other in their business like when AOL and Time Warner groups have declared their merger, they were eyeing on using each others competitiveness in delivering the services of both the companies together. Another reason for corporates lunching towards merger, to take advantage of taxation benefits, in which the strong firm get merged with sick firm and avail the tax benefits. But in such type of mergers also, the objective is that in long run the strong company is looking long term advantage of converting the sick unit as profit delivering arm of company in coming future by making effective changes in management practices, known as fundamental restructuring.

Acquisition

An acquisition, also known as a takeover, is the buying of one company (the 'target') by another. An acquisition may be friendly or hostile. In the former case, the companies cooperate in negotiations; in the latter case, the takeover target is unwilling to be bought or the target's board has no prior knowledge of the offer. Acquisition usually refers to a purchase of a smaller firm by a larger one. Sometimes, however, a smaller firm will acquire management control of a larger or longer established company and keep its name for the combined entity. This is known as a reverse takeover.

Section 395 of the Companies Act, 1956 provides the basic guidelines for acquiring an Indian company by another Indian company. While overseas acquisitions would be governed by the Takeover regulations applicable in the country where the target company is situate.

Emerging Trend and its Effect

The overseas acquisitions, which started off on a small scale, have reached to globally visible levels with big ticket acquisitions being announced by large corporates regularly. Tata group, Bharat Forge, Infosys, Wipro, ONGC, Ranbaxy and such Indian companies are venturing overseas and expanding at breakneck speed. The effect of this trend on the Indian economy has been rightly summarized by the Financ Minister Mr. P. Chidambaram—"Indian industry today has the confidence to bid for business abroad, raise resources, purchase and manage enterprises." Strategic investments continued to dominate M&A activity in 2007 with a share of 82 per cent in the total deal value, highlighting a growth of over two times over the same period in the previous year.

The dominance of the IT sector was challenged in the Indian M&A space by telecom, which accounted for 43 per cent of the total deal value, due to a small number of large deals. Finance and oil & gas, accounting for 15 per cent and 6 per cent of deal value respectively, emerged as favorite choices for investment outpacing the traditional sectors such as engineering, cement, power, etc.

Telecom: 4 deals, totalling Rs. 449 billion ($11 billion): The growing signs of consolidation towards the end of 2006 were more evident this year with Vodafone acquiring a 67

Sectors, Key deals

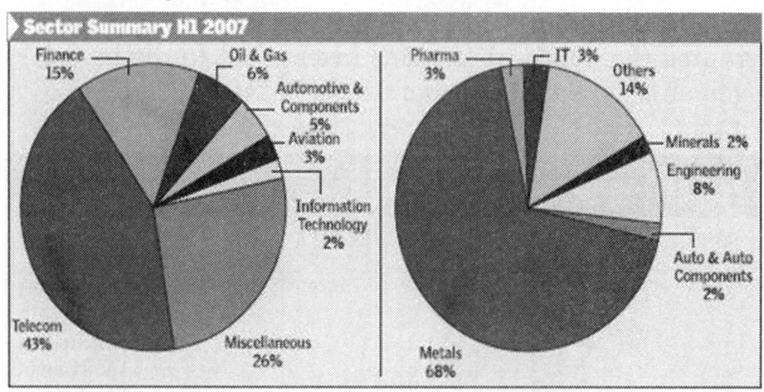

Source: www.business-world.co.in

per cent stake in Hutchison Essar, India's fourth largest telecom player. This deal took about three months to reach its conclusion with 5-6 contenders in the fray, ranging from the Anil Ambani controlled Reliance Infocomm to Orascom from Egypt and Maxis from Malaysia. Analysts were kept guessing at the valuations each day until Vodafone's final winning bid of Rs. 447 billion ($10.9 billion). Vodafone had earlier cleared the way for this deal in 2003 by selling its stake in the RPG Group controlled cellular telecom business.

Finance: 65 deals, totalling Rs. 157 billion ($4 billion): The Indian financial services (banking, insurance, and financial services) continue to attract overseas and domestic investors. The value of strategic deals has been slightly higher than PE investments in this segment. The majority of the deals were in the areas of broking, advisory, assets management and banking. During the period, various banks and financial institutions bought stakes in two leading bourses of the country—BSE and NSE—after these exchanges were de-metalized by the market regulator, SEBI (Securities and Exchange Board of India). The largest deal in this sector was the sale to investors such as Goldman Sachs, General Atlantic and Softbank Asia Infrastructure Fund of a 5.9 per cent stake in ICICI Financial Services (IFS) for Rs. 26.5 billion ($646 million). IFS will house the insurance, asset management and broking businesses of the ICICI Bank group. However, the Government has not yet granted the approvals for this investment to the investors even after repeated consideration.

Top deal - Overseas Targets

Deal Value in US$ mn	*Acquirer*	*Target*	*Equity Stake acquirer (%)*	*Acquirer Advisor advisor*	*Target / Seller*
12, 100	Tata Steel	Corus Plc	100	ABN Amro, Deutsche Bank, Rothchild	CSFB, JP Morgan, Cazenove, HSBC Securities and Capital Maket
3,500	Hindalco Industries	Novelis	100	UBS	-
1,794	Suzion Energy	Repower Systems AG	100	Yes Bank, ABN Amro	-
1,636	Essar Global	Algoma Steel Inc.	100	UBS	Genuity Capital Markets
1,177	United Spirits	Whyte & Mackay	100 100	UBS, ICIC Bank and Standard Chartered	Citigroup

Source: www.business-world.co.in

Oil & Gas: 5 deals, totalling Rs. 59 billion ($1.4 billion): The Mukesh Ambani controlled Reliance Industries dominated the M&A activity in the sector with two large deals accounting for almost the entire deal value in this sector. Mr. Mukesh Ambani, along with associates, increased his stake in the Group's flagship company, Reliance Industries Ltd. through an issue of convertible warrants. Upon conversion of instruments the promoters will control an additional 5 per cent stake.

Another significant deal in this sector was the merger of Indian Petrochemicals Corporation Ltd. (IPCL) into Reliance Industries, valued at Rs. 42 billion ($1 billion). IPCL came into the Reliance stable in 2002 when the government divested its 26 per cent stake and thereafter, Reliance increased it to 46 per cent through a tender offer. With this merger, the Reliance group has strengthened its market standing in the petrochemicals business, in which it is already the largest player.

Information Technology: 56 deals, totalling Rs. 25 billion ($604 million): The IT sector saw a slowdown in the M&A activity with total deal value accounting for less than 5 per cent for the first time since the last three years. This may also indicate a growing concern that IT is no longer an attractive sector for foreign investors as business models mature. The average deal size for this sector is Rs 442 million ($11 million).

The two significant deals were the sale of stakes by HDFC and Barclays in Intelenet, to the Blackstone Group along with the management for $86 million, and the purchase by WNS of a 100 per cent stake in Marketics Technologies, another BPO company.

Other Sectors: 169 deals, totalling Rs. 252 billion ($6 billion): Other sectors, including chemicals, construction, electronics, engineering, real estate, foods, hospitality, retailing and power, accounted for 24 per cent of the total deal value. Apart from these sectors, the auto sector (automotive and auto components) accounted for 5 per cent of the total deal value. The big deals in this sector were Robert Bosch gaining control over its Indian subsidiary through a delisting offer and M&M buying over Punjab Tractors for Rs. 14 billion ($350 million).

Other traditional sectors such as pharmaceuticals, textiles and cements contributed about 1 per cent each to the total deal value. The Indian aviation sector also saw many deals, contributing to about 3 per cent to the total deal value. This sector has been in the news since the entry of many low-cost carriers (LCCs) and has witnessed consolidation during 2007.

Jet Airways, India's largest private sector airline, took over Sahara, another large private sector player and the Vijay Mallya controlled Kingfisher Airlines acquiring a significant stake in India's first LCC, Deccan Aviation. The two state-owned carriers Indian Airline and Air India have announced the merger of their operations.

Overseas deals

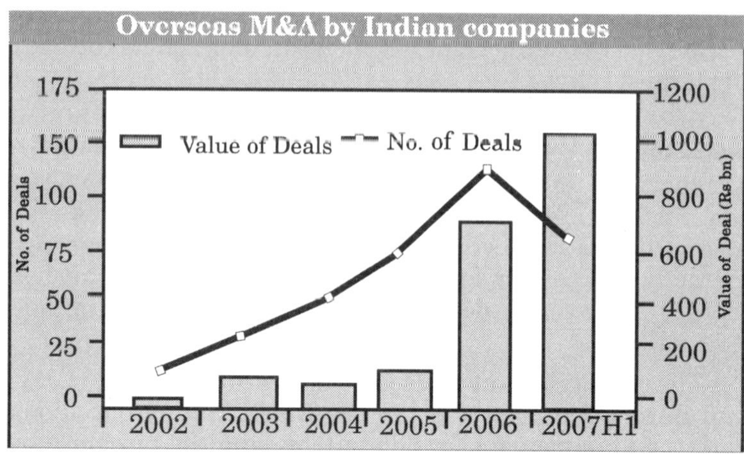

Source: www.business-world.co.in

Indian companies confirmed their presence on the global stage by announcing some of the largest deals in the history of Indian M&A. Indian companies now have the capability to acquire global companies that are much larger than themselves.

This period saw the much talked about Tata-Corus deal ($12.1 billion) finally consummated, followed by the Hindalco-Novelis deal ($3.5 billion). These two large deals accounted for 61 per cent of the total overseas deal value. The Tata-Corus deal catapulted Tata Steel to the 5th position in global ranking in steel from the mid-50s position it had before the acquisition. The Novelis deal will make Hindalco the world's largest aluminium rolling company. The significant aspect of these two deals is that both acquirers have realized that global consolidation is the only way to realize their growth strategy. They not only needed to acquire the global capacity but also to have access to overseas markets to achieve large scale operations and global competitiveness.

Conclusion

If one were to go by the signs of growth registered by Indian Corporates, it appears that in future more Indian companies will be charting their goals globally, both strategically and opportunistically. This is likely to lead to further overseas deals from India, providing building blocks to Indian corporates to emerge as large, competitive, global players. While some are yet to take notice of India Inc., it has already taken major steps in emerging as an economic superpower. So, we can say that nowdays are over, when MNCs can only dominate the business, it is our own Indian companies can also make a leap forward and prove themselves with the success for many Indian corporate houses like Tata, Hindalco and Essel Group, etc. So, let the globe be our business platform rather than only the country of origin.

References

1. Keynote address by Smt. Shyamala Gopinath, Deputy Governor, Reserve Bank of India, "Overseas Investments by Indian Companies-Evolution of Policy and Trends", on the Internet and World Wide Web.
2. www.wikipedia.org
3. www.business-world.co.in

7

Corporate Governance in Banks

Dr. Santosh Singh Bais
Mr. Srinivas Ranoor

ABSTRACT

In the age of competitive Globalization and dynamic world, business enterprises need to focus on innovative practices which will help in maximizing stake and shareholders wealth. The fundamental concern of corporate governance is to ensure that the firm's directors and managers act ethically in the interests of the firm and its shareholders and that the managers are held accountable to capital providers for the use of assets. The concept of Corporate Governance can be taken as a parallel to the quality practices under the ISO standard. It also involves entry of non-executive directors into the board, and making the members more positive and dynamic in their activities. All business information must be made available to them, and system controls are activated to ensure authenticity, timeliness and effectiveness of information. Globalization and Liberalization have taken the Indian corporate world towards the international field. This, not only is there a need to establish viable and acceptable corporate governance, but it should also conform to international standards. The basic principles of corporate governance are based on ethical parameters such as complete transparency, integrity and accountability.

Key Words: Corporate, Control, System, Ethics, Statutory, principles

Introduction

Indian banking has around 200 years of history and has undergone many transformations since independence. But, Liberalisation, Privatisation and Globalisation and Information Technology are currently changing the Indian banking radically. Earlier, banking was virtually a monopoly of the public sector banks with full protection from the State. But the process of reforms in the Indian banking system has thrown them out to more liberal and free market forces. Now the banks, more particularly the public sector ones, feel the real heat of the competition. The interest rate cuts, dwindling margins and more number of players to serve a reduced number of bankable clients have all added to the worries of the banks. The customer has finally come to hold the center stage and all banking products are tailor-made to suit his tastes and preferences. This sudden change in the banking environment has bereaved the banks of all their comforts and many of them are finding it extremely difficult to cope with the change.

Need for Corporate Governance in Banks

Since banks are important players in the Indian financial system, special focus on the Corporate Governance in the banking sector becomes critical. The Reserve Bank of India, as a regulator, has the responsibility on the nature of Corporate Governance in the banking sector. To the extent that banks have systemic implications, Corporate Governance in the banks is of critical importance. Given the dominance of public ownership in the banking system in India, corporate practices in the banking sector would also set the standards for Corporate Governance in the private sector. With a view to reducing the possible fiscal burden of recapitalizing the PSBs, attention towards Corporate Governance in the banking sector assumes added importance. The banking sector is not necessarily totally corporate. Some part of it is, of course, but a segment of banks is mostly government owned as statutory corporations or run as cooperatives – just like your b ank. Banking as a sector has been unique and the interests of other stake holders appear more important to it than in the case of non-banking and non-finance organisations. In the case of traditional manufacturing corporations, the issue has been that of safeguarding and maximising the shareholders' value. In the case of banking, the risk involved for depositors and the possibility of contagion assumes greater importance than that of consumers of manufactured products. Further, the involvement of government is discernibly higher in banks due to importance of stability of financial system and the larger interests of the public. Since the market control is not sufficient to ensure proper governance in banks, the government does see reason in regulating and controlling the nature of activities, the structure of bonds, the ownership pattern, capital adequacy norms, liquidity ratios, etc.

Reasons for High Degree of Oversight

There are three reasons for degree of government oversight in this sector.

- Firstly, it is believed that the depositors, particularly retail depositors, cannot effectively protect themselves as they do not have adequate information, nor are they in a position to coordinate with each other.
- Secondly, bank assets are unusually opaque, and lack transparency as well as liquidity. This condition arises due to the fact that most bank loans, unlike other products and services, are usually customised and privately negotiated.

Thirdly, it is believed that there could be a contagion effect resulting from the instability of one bank, which would affect a class of banks or even the entire financial system and the economy. As one bank becomes unstable, there may be a heightened perception of risk among depositors for the entire class of such banks, resulting in a run on the deposits and putting the entire financial system in jeopardy.

Genesis of Corporate Governance

It will certainly not be out of place here to recount how issues relating to corporate governance and corporate control have come to the fore the world over in the recent past. The seeds of modern corporate governance were probably sown by the Watergate scandal in the USA. Subsequent investigations by US regulatory and legislative bodies highlighted control failures that had allowed several major corporations to make illegal political contributions and bribe government officials. While these developments in the US stimulated debate in the UK, a spate of scandals and collapses in that country in the late 1980s and early 1990s led shareholders and banks to worry about their investments. Several companies in UK which saw explosive growth in earnings in the '80s ended the decade in a memorably disastrous manner. Importantly, such spectacular corporate failures arose primarily out of poorly managed business practices.

This debate was driven partly by the subsequent enquiries into corporate governance (most notably the Cadbury Report) and partly by extensive changes in corporate structure. In May 1991, the London Stock Exchange set up a Committee under the chairmanship of Sir Arian Cadbury to help raise the standards of corporate governance and the level of confidence in financial reporting and auditing by setting out clearly what it sees as the respective responsibilities of those involved and what it believes is expected of them. The Committee investigated accountability of the Board of Directors to shareholders and to the society. It submitted its report and the associated 'Code of Best Practices' in December 1992 wherein it spelt out the methods of governance needed to achieve a balance between the essential powers of the Board of Directors and their proper accountability. Being a pioneering report on corporate governance, it would perhaps be in order to make a brief reference to its recommendations which are in the nature of guidelines relating to, among other things, the Board of Directors and Reporting & Control.

The Cadbury Report stipulated that the Board of Directors should meet regularly, retain full and effective control over the company and monitor the executive management. There should be a clearly accepted division of responsibilities at the head of the company which will ensure balance of power and authority so that no individual has unfettered powers of decision. The Board should have a formal schedule of matters specifically reserved to it for decisions to ensure that the direction and control of the company is firmly in its hands. There should also be an agreed procedure for Directors in the furtherance of their duties to take independent professional advice.

The Cadbury Report generated a lot of interest in India. The issue of corporate governance was studied in depth and dealt with by the Confederation of Indian Industries (CII), Associated Chamber of Commerce and Industry (ASSOCHAM) and Securities and Exchange Board of India (SEBI). These studies reinforced the Cadbury Report's focus on the crucial role of the Board and the need for it to observe a Code of Best Practices. Co-operative banks as corporate entities possess certain unique characteristics. Paradoxical as it may sound, evolution of co-operatives in India as peoples' organisations rather than business enterprises adopting professional managerial systems has hindered growth of professionalism in co-operatives and proved to be a neglected area in their evolution.

Essential Governance Principles

The Basel Committee has issued several papers on specific topics. These include "Framework for internal control systems in banking organizations" (September, 1998) "Enhancing Bank Transparency" and Principles for the management of credit risk (July, 1999). The following are the practices to avoid governance problems.

1. The Company should lay solid foundations for management and oversight, recognize and publish the respective roles and responsibilities of board and management.

2. Structure the board to add value: have a board of an effective composition, size and commitment to adequately discharge its responsibilities and duties.
3. Actively promote ethical and responsible decision-making.
4. Safeguard integrity and financial reporting: have a structure to independently verify and safeguard the integrity of the company's financial reporting.
5. Make timely and balanced disclosure of all material matters concerning the company.
6. Respect the rights of the shareholders and facilitate the effective exercise of those rights.
7. Recognize and manage risk through system of risk oversight and management and internal control.
8. Fairly review and encourage enhanced performance.
9. Remunerate fairly and responsibly and its relationship to corporate and individual performance is defined.
10. Recognize the legitimate interests of stakeholders.
11. Corporate governance rating be made mandatory for listed companies.
12. Ensure that the board members are well qualified and not subject to pressure.
13. Ethical Approach: A clearly ethical basis to the business.
14. Conducting corporate governance in a transparent manner.

Measures taken by Banks towards Implementation of Best Practices

Prudential norms in terms of income recognition, asset classification, and capital adequacy have been well assimilated by the Indian banking system. In keeping with the international best practice, starting 31st March 2004, banks have adopted 90 days norm for classification of NPAs. Also, norms governing provisioning requirements in respect of doubtful assets have been made more stringent in a phased manner. Beginning 2005, banks will be required to set aside capital charge for market risk on their trading portfolio of government investments, which was earlier virtually exempt from market risk requirement.

Capital Adequacy: All the Indian banks barring one today are well above the stipulated benchmark of 9 per cent and remain in a state of preparedness to achieve the best standards of CRAR as soon as the new Basel 2 norms are made operational. In fact, as of 31st March 2004, banking system as a whole had a CRAR close to 13 per cent.

On the Income Recognition Front, there is complete uniformity now in the banking industry and the system therefore ensures responsibility and accountability on the part of the management in proper accounting of income as well as loan impairment.

ALM and Risk Management Practices: At the initiative of the regulators, banks were quickly required to address the need for Asset Liability Management followed by risk management practices. Both these are critical areas for an effective oversight by the Board and the senior management which are implemented by the Indian banking system on a tight time frame and the implementation review by RBI. These steps have enabled banks to understand, measure and anticipate the impact of the interest rate risk and liquidity risk, which in deregulated environment is gaining importance.

Measures taken by Regulator towards Corporate Governance

Reserve Bank of India has taken various steps furthering corporate governance in the Indian Banking System. These can broadly be classified into the following three categories: (a) Transparency (b) Off-site surveillance (c) Prompt corrective action. *Transparency* and disclosure standards are also important constituents of a sound corporate governance mechanism. Transparency and accounting standards in India have been enhanced to align with international best practices. However, there are many gaps in the disclosures in India vis-à-vis the international standards, particularly in the area of risk management strategies and risk parameters, risk concentrations, performance measures, component of capital structure, etc. Hence, the disclosure standards need to be further broad-based in consonance with improvements in the capability of market players to analyse the information objectively.

The *off-site surveillance* mechanism is also active in monitoring the movement of assets, its impact on capital adequacy and overall efficiency and adequacy of managerial practices in banks. RBI also brings out the periodic data on "Peer Group Comparison" on critical ratios to maintain peer pressure for better performance and governance.

Prompt corrective action has been adopted by RBI as a part of core principles for effective banking supervision. As against a single trigger point based on capital adequacy normally adopted by many countries, Reserve Bank in keeping with Indian conditions have set two more trigger points namely Non-Performing Assets (NPA) and Return on Assets (ROA) as proxies for asset quality and profitability. These trigger points will enable the intervention of regulator through a set of mandatory action to stem further deterioration in the health of banks showing signs of weakness.

Conclusion

In the years to come, the Indian financial system will grow not only in size but also in complexity as the forces of competition gain further momentum and financial markets acquire greater depth. The policy environment will remain supportive of healthy growth and development with accent on more operational flexibility as well as greater prudential regulation and supervision. The real success of our financial sector reforms will however depend primarily on the organisational effectiveness of the banks. Corporate Governance has assumed vital role and significance due to globalisation and liberalisation. With the opening of economy and to be in line with WTO requirements, if the Indian corporates have to survive and succeed amidst increasing competition globally, it can only be through transparency in operations. The excellence in terms of customer satisfaction, in terms of return, in terms of product and service, in terms of return to promoters and in terms of social responsibilities towards society and people cannot be achieved without practicing good Corporate Governance. With elements of good corporate governance, sound investment policy, appropriate internal control systems, better credit risk management, focus on newly-emerging business areas like micro finance, commitment to better customer service, adequate automation and proactive policies on house-keeping issues, co-operative banks will definitely be able to grapple with these challenges and convert them into opportunities.

References

1. "Corporate Governance in Public Sector Banks—Issue and Challenges" by Ambika Prasad Pati and Vijaykumar, *Journal of Accounting and Finance,* Vol. 19, No.1 October-2004 and March-2005.
2. Opening address delivered by J.J Irani, Subir Raha and Suresh Prabha on "Corporate and Public Governance" on November 29, 2005 during the conference held at IIM-Ahmedabad.
3. Jones, Randall S. Tsuru, Kotaro, "Japan Corporate Governance: A System in Evolution" *OECD Observer*, Issue 204, February-March 1997, pp. 40-41.
4. *Productivity Promotion,* vol. 10 No. 36.
5. *New Dimensions in Global Business Perspective-2001,* Edited by B. Bhattacharyya, Excel Book, New-Delhi, 1998.
6. J.J. Irani Committee Report on Company Law related to Corporate Governance by S.C Das, The Management Accountant, September 2005.
7. Corporate Governance by H. Narayanan Retd. Chief (PR and Publicity) *Yogakshema,* vol.45, No.11, November-2001.
8. The Working Group on Corporate Governance, "A New Compact for Owners and Directors", *Harward Business Review,* July-August 1991 pp. 141-143.
9. Boyd Colin, "Ethics and Corporate Governance: The Issues Raised by the Cadbury Report in the United Kingdom", *Journal of Business Ethics* vol.15, Issue 2, February-11, 96 pp. 167-182.

10. Corporate Governance in the United Kingdom: The Rise of Fiduciary Capitalism—A review of literature by James P Hawley and Andrew T. Williams, LENS inc's Internet Site.

11. Bhide and Amar, "Efficient Market, Deficient Governance", *Harward Business Review,* November-December 1994, pp. No. 128-139.

8

Role of Independent Directors in Good Corporate Governance in India

Prof. Trilok Nath Shukla
Prof. Chumki Chatterjee

ABSTRACT

In a recent article in *Business Today,* several well-renowned people accepted that they had joined as an ID as the company belonged to an old friend! How can one even expect them to be disloyal to their friends in the boardroom? In India, the Companies Act, 1956, being more than half a century old with most of the sections being dormant or obsolete and handful of changes brought about through amendments in the existing framework, it is high time that we go for a new and competent framework. However, due to political instability and lethargic attitudes of politicians, this important legislation is staggering between parliamentary sessions since the last few years. Since Independent Directors are handpicked by the promoters himself so they prefer to be a friend of the promoters rather than be the watchdog of the board. Satyam episode is proven to be tragic for the Indian corporate world, but it should be considered as a wake-up call to many. The Satyam case brought out the failure of the present corporate governance structure, in which independent directors failed to perform their responsibility effectively. It has demonstrated that even highly credible, qualified and educated persons are no insurance for corporate governance, that they are not independent of the promoters, providing blind support to them, and that they are no watchdogs of the minority shareholders whose interests they are supposed to serve. There is no need to implement new laws; all we need to do is to renew existing laws.

Introduction

The concept of "Independent Directors" which initially begin as good corporate governance has now become, a mandatory element of corporate law. Across the world, it is widely accepted fact that, they are the answers to many problems but following every corporate collapse, the issue arises, how?

In India, the Companies Act, 1956, being more than half a century old with most of the sections being dormant or obsolete and handful of changes brought about through amendments in the existing framework, it is high time that we go for a new and competent framework. However, due to political instability and lethargic attitudes of politicians, this important legislation is staggering between parliamentary sessions since the last few years. It seems, as if, they are not in a mood to learn even from the Satyam fiasco that occurred lately. Following the disclosure of extensive accounting fraud by the promoter family in Satyam, several independent directors resigned from other Indian firms. Since these resignations were motivated by an unexpected shock external to the firm, they were unaffected by firm- and director-specific factors coinciding with the time of the resignation. Using the extraordinarily large number of such resignations in January 2009, we find the four-day cumulative abnormal return surrounding director resignations to be-1.3 per cent. Consistent with the monitoring role of independent directors, we find that the effect is disproportionately greater for those independent directors that sit on the audit committee and possess business expertise; while the effect of being in the audit committee is greater for smaller firms, the effect of business expertise is felt more in large firms. Finally, the departing independent directors are missed less in family owned firms.

Recessions typically reveal corporate governance transgressions, insider trading and fraud, all of which would implicate independent directors. But the fact that independent directors are not employed directly by the company, do not receive the salaries of executive directors, nor have any particular allegiance to it, suggests that they will be the first to leave. As someone not directly involved in the day-to-day running of the company, an independent director does not have access to the same information as executive directors and any access he or she does have is often dependent on goodwill from the board. But despite accusations of pliancy in some jurisdictions, the benefit of independent directors has been proven, especially in countries with a high proportion of family-owned businesses.

Definition and Meaning

The general definition of ID is "a non-executive director on the board of company, who has integrity, expertise and independence to balance the interest of various stakeholders". Higgs Report (2003) has provides a much clear definition of ID: "that a non-executive director is considered independent when the board determines that the director is independent in character and judgment and there are no relationships or circumstances which could affect, or appear to affect, the directors' judgment". As per Clause 49 of the Listing Agreements an 'independent director' shall mean non-executive director of the company who

- apart from receiving director's remuneration, does not have any material pecuniary relationships or transactions with the company, its promoters, its senior management or its holding company, its subsidiaries and associated companies.

- is not related to promoters or management at the board level or at one level below the board.
- has not been an executive of the company in the immediately preceding three financial years.
- is not a partner or an executive of the statutory audit firm or the internal audit firm that is associated with the company, and has not been a partner or an executive of any such firm for the last three years. This will also apply to legal firm(s) and consulting firm(s) that have a material association with the entity.
- is not a supplier, service provider or customer of the company. This should include lessor-lessee type relationships also; and
- is not a substantial shareholder of the company, i.e. owning two per cent or more of the block of voting shares.
- is over 21 years of age.

Objectives

The Higgs Report has described role of non-executive director (including ID) into two principal components: monitoring executive activity and contributing to the development of strategy. The main motive to have IDs on the board is to have check on management and ensuring that decisions align in direction of shareholders value. The main objective of keeping the independent directors are:

- Selected to provide specialist skill, counterbalancing management weakness in a company.
- Add diversity to the board, to change the culture of unitary board.
- Provide an independent appraisal—separation of ownership and control.
- Corporate experience and leadership qualities.
- To provide strategic oversight to company, providing the expertise.
- Status/credibility to governance model—to present the public face of the business

- As chairman—to provide leadership and vision.
- Protection of minorities.
- To build up shareholder's confidence in the company.
- To improve relations with investors.
- To resolve conflicts.
- To enhance management transparency.
- To increase company's value.
- Role of other stakeholders in management.
- System of reporting and accountability.
- Audit and internal control.
- To encourage Sustainable Development of the Company and its stakeholders.

Background

The genesis of actual IDs began only in 1970s, as part of CG reforms to fulfill the monitoring role. The position of IDs consolidated in the CG framework during hostile takeover period, with recognition of their role in enhancing shareholders prosperity. Subsequently, number of frauds in UK resulted in commissioning of Cadbury Committee on CG in 1992, which provided broadened definition of ID, their role and relation in the company. In 1997, Hampel Committee (UK) and Blue Ribbon Committee (US), further defined and enhanced the role of IDs.

The paradigm shift however, occurred after number of corporate failures like WorldCom and Enron, with passing of Sarbanes-Oxley (SOX) legislation. The act not only reinvented the role of ID but also made various corporate actions a necessity and increased the legal complexity. The SOX requires all the members of the audit committees to be independent with redefined roles and enforces strict penalties for any transgression. Higgs Report (2003) on effectiveness of non-executive directors and Smith Report (2005) on audit committees, after the happenings in US, provided a big thrust to concrete the position of IDs in CG framework of UK.

The Higgs Report particularly touched upon many aspects and proposed significant changes, redefined the independence and role of non-executive directors, particularly IDs in the corporate board of the company. NYSE comprehensively revised its listing standards after SOX, requiring majority of directors to be independent, and strict independence criteria applied to all such directors, not just the audit committees. In wake of the recent financial meltdown, the role of IDs is under critical analysis in the developed world. A number of reports in US and UK have looked upon the role of ID in the global financial crisis and pointed many flaws in the present system of IDs. They have stressed on need to strengthen the institution of IDs, so that they can play significant role in the avoiding failures of corporations.

Indian Scenario

The term "Independent Director" was first introduced in the Indian corporate arena through the Kumar Mangalam Birla Committee, formulated by SEBI, to start up reforms in the area of CG. It soon found entry into corporate books, after Clause 49 was incorporated in Listing Agreement by SEBI. In the background of Enron debacle and sequel to SOX in US, Ministry of Company Affairs (MCA, then known as DCA) then constituted, the Naresh Chandra Committee, which gave governance some more thought. Committee recommended IDs should not be less than fifty per cent of the board. Nominee directors of lending institutions not be considered as independents. The recommendations encompassing the audit committees were identical to those of SOX, requiring all members of committee to be independent and having written charter for its function. It also provided impetus to ID remuneration, training and recommended to exempt them from criminal and civil liabilities. In 2003, SEBI constituted the Narayana Murthy Committee with terms overlapping with that of Chandra Committee, whose recommendations were incorporated in the Clause 49 by amending it in 2004.

The Murthy report adopted the same definition of IDs as formulated by the Chandra Committee, however, without the condition of nine-year term. It also pondered the view on the qualification and remuneration of IDs and stressed on the need for evaluating performance of non-executive directors. Sequel to implementation of Murthy Committee recommendation in Clause 49, MCA constituted another committee in December 2004 under the Chairmanship of Shri J. J. Irani, to give CG a legislative stamp by revamping the Companies Act, 1956. The Irani Committee came up with several recommendations that were in conflict with the extant Clause 49 and/or the views of the Murthy Committee, e.g. (a) providing for several exemptions based on size and extent of public ownership in a mandatory CG framework so as to optimize compliance costs while maintaining a desired level of regulatory rigour; (b) the criteria for "independence" of IDs is proposed to be weakened significantly; (c) the mandatory requirement of IDs to constitute one-half of the Board be weakened to one-third of the total members of the Boards, (d) abolition of age limits for IDs. The present CG framework encompassing the ID is through Clause 49 based on the Murthy Report.

However Satyam's accounting scandal increased the pressure on independent directors, and in turn, raised fears that directorships would be harder to fill. India's independent directors are often appointed by controlling shareholders and some fear they may owe a debt of responsibility to those shareholders. As it stands today, the existing company law has no mention of independent directors. They can't magically prohibit the scams from happening in a company; the very purpose behind appointing independent directors is to put checks and balances on each and every activity of the company and bring independence, impartiality and wide experience. It has been decided in *Central Government* vs. *Sterling Holiday Resorts (India) Ltd. and Ors.* that "the Board of directors should be strengthened by appointing independent directors." One possible solution to this lies in mandatory nomination committees. Although there is no requirement to have nomination committees, several companies such as Infosys, an IT company, have established them voluntarily. Umakanth Varottil, a former lawyer at Amarchand Mangaldas Suresh A Shroff & Co. says that doing so would instil greater independence of directors from controlling shareholders, and more allegiance to minority investors.

Companies Act and Independent Directors

The Companies Act looks at all directors alike:

- Throws some extra compliances in case of whole time directors.
- Requires some disclosures by interested directors.
- Defines "officer in default" giving a degree of immunity to directors other than the whole time directors.
- Does not exempt independent directors from any of the duties, liabilities, responsibilities of the Board.

Legal Provisions

- Sec 5: officer in default: Independent directors are treated as such only where the company does not have a wholetime director, or no specific director is charged with a particular compliance: this provision is not applicable for compliances under any other law.
- Sec 267-269: applicable only to wholetime directors.
- Sec 274: applicable to all directors.
- Sec 284: procedure for removal of directors applicable to all directors.
- Sec 291: general powers exercisable through board meetings.
- Sec 292: certain powers may be delegated to wholetime directors.
- Sec 292A: composition of the audit committee to include a majority of directors other than wholetime directors.
- Sec 297, 299, 300: applicable to all directors.
- Sec. 309 (4): Separate limits and restrictions applicable on remuneration of independent directors.

- Explanation IV to Schedule XIII: Managerial remuneration: Appointment and remuneration of managerial personnel to be decided upon by the remuneration committee. Committee to consist of at least 3 non-executive independent directors.

Independent Directors under Listing Agreement in India

Committees of Directors

Audit Committee: requirements other than those u/s 292A shall have minimum 3 members, all of them being non-executive and majority of them being independent.

- Chairman of the committee shall be an independent director
- To meet at least thrice a year
- Company Secretary to act as secretary to the committee
- Remuneration Committee
- Shareholders/Investors Grievance Committee
- Limits on committee memberships and chairmanships

Liabilities under Other Laws

- The basic directorial liability apart, being a corporate director may invite liabilities under myriad Central, State and Local laws:
- Most often, notices, summons, etc are addressed to all directors.
- Sometimes, IT searches are also unable to distinguish between working directors and independent directors.

Recent Examples of Liabilities of Independent Directors

- In case of Worldcom and Enron, directors settled liabilities:

  $ 18 million by 10 outside directors in Worldcom

  $ 13 million by 10 directors in Enron
- In Walt Disney case, the court did not impose liability on directors.

- The conclusion is inevitable that the liability arises on account of conduct, act or omission on the part of a person and not merely on account of holding an office or a position in a company. SC ruling in *SMS Pharmaceuticals Ltd.,* Sept 2005:
- On one hand, independent directors can be arrested for minor offences—offences that they are not even connected to, like bounced company cheques, late employee provident fund payments, even though they do not manage the company. On the other hand, there is no law—Company, SEBI or otherwise, that defines the responsibility of independent directors and hence their accountability. Of course, fraud or collusion in fraud is punishable under the criminal code, but there is no booking negligence. Which means, independent directors with a silent conscience—those who turn a blind eye to mismanagement, can escape without punishment.

A Basic Design of Existing Corporate Governance Systems

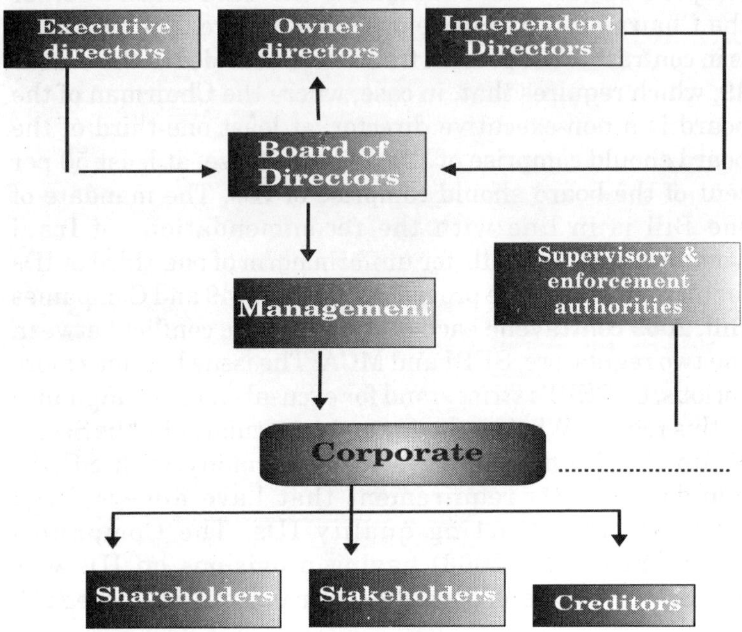

Independent Directors in the light of the Companies Bill, 2009

The IDs for the first time have entered into statue books of Indian legislation with the introduction of Companies Bill 2009. MCA (Ministry of Corporate affairs) in concurrence with submission of the Irani Report in 2005 has started the process of revamping the Companies Act, 1956. The efforts culminated in the introduction of the Companies Bill, 2008 in the 14th Lok Sabha on October 23, 2008. The bill was subsequently referred to the appropriate Parliamentary Standing Committee on Finance for examination and report. Before the said Committee could present its report, 14th Lok Sabha was dissolved and the Companies Bill, 2008 lapsed under the provisions of clause (5) of Article 107 of the Constitution of India. In view of this, the Companies Bill, 2009 has been introduced in Parliament on August 3, 2009.

(a) Board Composition: The Companies Bill, 2009, through Clause 132(3) prescribes that board of all listed companies should have mandatory one-third of IDs whether the Chairman is executive or non-executive. The provision is in contrast to the present framework provided in the Clause 49, which requires that, in case, where the Chairman of the board is a non-executive director, at least one-third of the board should comprise of IDs and otherwise, at least 50 per cent of the board should comprise of IDs. The mandate of the Bill is in line with the recommendations of Irani Committee, which calls for uniform norm of one-third of IDs for all companies. The provisions of Clause 49 and Companies Bill, 2009 contravene each other, and raise conflict between the two regulators, SEBI and MCA. The issue becomes more serious, on SEBI's strict stand for excusal on non-compliance in this regard. Whole industry and particularly Public Sector Units (PSUs) have always in disharmony with SEBI's mandate on IDs requirement that have always faced difficulty in attracting quality IDs. The Companies Amendment Bill (2003) having provisions on IDs was withdrawn due to stiff opposition from industry in this regard.

The PSUs have long demanded that nominee directors appointed by government to be treated as ID, as an alternative. The Clause 132 of the proposed Bill is in line with their demand, though it needs to be regulated through the SEBI and stock exchanges. Nominee directors are excluded from the IDs. This is in concordance with SEBI stance to treat them at par with normal directors.

(b) Defining Independence: Clause 132(5) lays the definition of ID similar to that of framework provided in Clause 49; however, both have certain inadequacies. The Bill defines ID as "a non-executive director who in opinion of the board is a person of integrity and experience and poses relevant experience and expertise". While Clause 49 of Listing Agreement fixes the minimum age for the ID to be 21 years, the Clause 132 of the Bill does not prescribes so, in analogy with Irani Committee commendations. However, this contravenes with primary definition of ID itself, how a person who even does not possess a graduate degree (person below 21 years) can bring expertise and experience, and much more that an independent thinking on the board that can help company in achieving its objective.

The Bill while defining ID, also states that IDs (or their relatives) should not have pecuniary relationship or transactions with company, its holding, subsidiary or associate company, or its directors amounting to 10 per cent or more of its gross turnover or total income during the two immediately preceding financial years or during the current financial years. The turnover of companies has now reached thousand of crores and if director is having transaction in hundred of crores, the foremost question that arises is, will he truly be independent in genuine sense. Permitting an ID to have financial transactions with company up to such a large extent has potential of conflict of interest.

(c) Retiring Age: The Bill prescribes maximum age limit for key managerial personnel to retire at the age of 70, however on the bases of Irani Report, for IDs, no retiring age is stipulated. Earlier, DCA on the bases of Joshi Committee

(1997) in Companies Amendment Act, 2003 proposed to a have retiring age for director by inserting new section 280 in Companies Act, 1956, which stipulates that no person shall be eligible to hold office as MD/ WTD or other director or manager of company if he has attained the age of 75 years.

(d) Qualification and Experience: The Companies Bill, 2009 does not necessitate ID to possess any educational qualification and experience. Even Clause 49 and present Act not requires so. According to Clause 132(5), any person can be appointed as ID:

(a) who, in the opinion of the Board, is a person of integrity and possesses relevant expertise and experience;

(b) who possesses such other qualifications as may be prescribed. In both, present Act as well the Bill, only the disqualifications and conditions that does not allow any person to become an ID.

It is high time for Indian legislatures and corporates to have debate on this issue, as this is one major reason for the recent financial crisis, quoted by many reports of developed world.

(e) Appointments: Clause 133 of the Bill, which corresponds to the sections 254, 255 and 264 of the Companies Act, 1956, lays down how directors including ID would be appointed. The Clause 133, provisions are analogous to present Act—every director other than first directors will be appointed in general meeting of company, after furnishing DIN and declaration for non-disqualification. In addition, clause also requires board to give a report in the general meeting that every ID appointed fulfils the conditions specified for his appointment. The Clause 49 in similar manner prescribes the appointment of IDs.

It is established fact that most of the Indian companies are family controlled, further marked by cross-holdings, pyramid structures and tunnelling. According to a study of broad base BSE 500 set of companies, "the average promoter owns roughly 49 per cent, and fewer than 9 per cent of promoters have stakes below 25 per cent". Independent directors have to owe their loyalty to promoters for appointments and their continuation. If the Indian legislators in reality want to have ID on the board, the whole practice of appointing needs to be given a fresh glance while getting in to root cause of the problem

(f) Remuneration: The remuneration that can be paid to the ID is given by Clause 132(6), according to which an ID is not entitled to any remuneration, other than sitting fee, reimbursement of expenses for participation in the board and other meetings and profit-related commission and stock options as may be approved by the members. Further, clause 176 (1), that corresponds to existing Section 309 of Companies Act, specifies that any director who is neither WTD (Working Time Directive) or MD can be paid remuneration only in the form of fee for attending board meeting and profit related commission. The Clause 176(2) also states that if any director draws or receives directly or indirectly by way of remuneration, any sum in excess of the amount under sub-section (1), he shall refund such sum to the company within thirty days. The Clause 49 prescribes that IDs can be paid any fee and stock options fixed by board with prior approval of shareholders in general meeting. As per current stipulation of Companies Act, an ID earn up to Rs. 10000 or Rs. 20000 depending upon company, as sitting fee for each meeting of board of committee thereof. Under Sec 309, commission to non-executive directors including independent, cannot exceed one per cent of net profit if company has MD/ WTD/ Manager, otherwise the limit is three per cent.

The new Bill now allows the company and its shareholders to fix sitting fees and profit related commission paid to IDs without any capping. As for stock options, there is no limit, just approval of board members.

(g) Term: The current Bill does not sets any fix term for IDs. They are eligible for re-appointment of the board after their term over, subject to board recommendation and shareholders approval in the general meeting of the company.

Clause 49 has non-mandatory requirements stipulates that ID after 9 years (3 terms of 3 years each) association with company will cease to independent.

(h) Number of Directorship: The Clause 146 of Bill that corresponds to the Section 275 of the Companies Act, no person can become director in more than fifteen public limited companies. The Clause 49, on the contrary mandates that a person can become member of ten committees or at maximum chair five and has to disclose his commitments with other companies in annual report of company. The Companies (Amendment) Act, 2000 previously reduced number of directorship from 20 to 15 a person can hold, but current Bill is liberal in not altering it.

(i) Duties/Responsibility/Liabilities: According to provisions of Clause 147 (3), an ID should exercise his duties with due and reasonable care, skill and diligence. The Clause 158, which corresponds to some provisions of the 292A of present Act, requires ID should form the majority and chair the audit and remuneration committee. Further, if we look at definition of "officer in default" provided in the Clause 2 (zzi) of the Bill corresponding to the Section 5 of the Companies Act, the IDs are included in same. By virtue provisions of same clause: "(vi) every director, in respect of a contravention of any of the provisions of this Act, who is aware of such contravention by virtue of the receipt by him of any proceedings of the board or participation in such proceedings without objecting to the same, or where such contravention had taken place with his consent or connivance".

In Companies Act, 1956, it can be observed that IDs are included in the definition of "Officer in default" under Section 5. However, the accused ID can be granted relief by court, if they can satisfactorily prove that they have performed their functions honestly and exercised it with due diligence, care and caution. The listed cases torch light on the discussed issue.

1. Supreme Court: *N.K. Wahi* vs *Sekhar Singh and others* (2007) 2 LJ 10 (SC);

2. Rajasthan High Court: *Alim Ahuja* vs *Registrar of Companies* (2005) 62 SCL 110 (Raj);
3. Supreme Court: *SMS Pharmaceuticals Limited* vs *Neeta Bhalla* [2005] 6 CLJ 144 (SC).

The Satyam fiasco has raised questions over the responsibilities and liabilities of the IDs. Serious Fraud Investigation Office (SFIO) has filed seven cases against eleven ex-directors (including IDs) of Satyam. Followed by this, AP government's move to arrest the ID of Nagarjuna Finance in alleged involvement of repayment of public deposits has worsened the situation. All this created a fear psychosis in the mind of ID. According to a report, nearly 340 IDs have resigned from their post. Many people are now not advent to accept the post of ID and tarnish their reputation.

Are Independent Directors Independent in India?

Since Independent Directors are handpicked by the promoters himself so they prefer to be a friend of the promoters rather than be the watchdog of the board. There are circumstances where independent directors are not independent, which broadly includes:

(a) Selection procedure: They cannot be as independent as they are expected to be, if they are going to be appointed by the owners. This procedure has to be changed for the independence of directors.

(b) No age limit: There is no age limit has been prescribed under Companies Act, 1956 and by the SEBI. Even a minor can become a director since no age limit is prescribed.

(c) No specific qualification is required: They should be qualified enough so that they can ask right questions at the right time when they are at board. They need to be sound in judgement with an inquiring mind. Clause 49 of the Listing Agreement of the stock exchanges and the Companies Bill, 2008 does not prescribe the minimum qualification or experience essential.

(d) No right to interfere in the day-to-day operations: They are supposed to support the management in getting the delivery of what the objectives of the company are to its shareholders. If a director cannot get into a company's day-to-day operations, he cannot understand how it is governed and will not be in the position to fulfill his responsibilities.

(e) No time limit for replacement of an independent director: There is no guideline prescribing a time limit for replacement of an independent director in case there is a resignation or removal or death of an existing one and promoters are taking a plea that they have not been able to find a replacement, which could stretch for indefinite period. The fees or remuneration of an independent director has grown so substantially in the last three years that an individual is often tempted to have an extended stay in the organization. To retain the independence of director there is need to rotate such directors periodically or by any other method whereby the independence of independent director is secured.

Drawbacks

IDs are mandated only for the listed companies, because these companies have raised money from the public. But the unlisted companies, which are over 8.60 lakh and some of them even larger than the largest of the listed firms, do not require IDs. So the only real meaning of "independent" is that such persons should be independent of the promoters (and the management, which incidentally in India is a combined position in most cases). IDs may have made some sense in the US, for example, where companies are widely held and where the undue enrichment of the CEOs had to be curtailed. In India, most companies are family-run. Requiring such families to induct IDs is debatable; giving these families the unbridled power of appointment of IDs defeats the very objective of independence. No promoter in his senses would invite a stranger on his board (and by the same logic, no person of any repute would expose himself to a strange company by accepting its directorship!). A board position provides huge access to company information, including confidential information, that a promoter may not feel comfortable giving to a stranger, for fear of misuse. An unknown quantity can also create impediments. Moreover, most promoters have too much to hide and they often resort to window dressing, something that would not be possible with a stranger around. Little wonder, the home directors' category is the most overwhelming one. Several loopholes exist to get home people on boards. For example, according to the Companies Act, all persons from the wife's and mother's side are not considered as relatives. So a company can get on its board, for example, the promoter's father-in-law or wife's brother or mother's brother and call him independent!

An analysis of educational qualifications of the IDs reveals that most IDs do not, even understand the basics of finance, and have no noteworthy corporate qualification or experience. Ask them questions about balance sheets, profit and loss account, sundry debtors, sundry creditors, forex hedging or accounting standards, and they would be embarrassed! Worse, many of them have never invested in the equity markets, and they actually proudly proclaim so. If financial gain for ID is taken into account then it is a known fact that each meeting of the board or a committee can fetch an ID Rs. 20,000. On top of this, the law allows one per cent of profits to be distributed among the IDs. Furthermore, there is no limit on ESOPs that can be granted to the IDs. Then an ID can be on the boards of subsidiary companies and derive remuneration from there. Finally, expenses on travel, boarding and lodging etc. can be substantial. There are also examples of board meetings being convened only for allowing an ID to undertake travel. A study currently under process by Prime reveals the huge payouts being made to IDs. The best case is of a retired bureaucrat who earned a royal sum of Rs. 2.20 crore in 2007-08 as an ID. This fee came from 10 listed companies and 2 foreign companies, but excludes remuneration from 4 unlisted companies (a couple of these being very large firms), which could have paid big sums too. The remuneration data captured by Prime is based only on the official disclosures in the annual reports. It is widely believed that, in addition, there are cash payments, payments in kind and payments to front entities of the IDs.

The directors database.com reveals that there are hundreds of individuals who hold directorships in a large number of companies (as many as 330 individuals hold 5 or more than 5 directorship positions in listed companies, and in addition, directorships of several unlisted companies). The Companies Act puts a ceiling of 15 directorships of public companies. However, among public companies, it is beyond debate that the listed ones demands a much greater degree of commitment from an ID, including attending at least four board meetings and several meetings of one or more of the many committees during a year. How many of such IDs can play an effective role in the listed companies is a moot question.

Several senior government officials have accepted ID positions post-retirement. Is there not a question of propriety in being a director of a company that one had regulated just some time back or which would get listed in the future? Only 2.5 per cent of IDs are women (162 out of 6,443). The directorsdatabase.com had earlier revealed that many kids (even 18 year olds) were on boards of companies as IDs. While arguably the son of a promoter-director can be of such an age, someone so young surely cannot acquire enough experience to become an ID of another company. However, SEBI has now mandated 21 years; the logic being that one can contest the parliament election at that age. But then to become an MP, one has to at least get elected. It is true that the shareholders have to elect a director too, but the farce of shareholders' meetings is well known; the IDs are pure nominees of the promoters. Presently, there are as many as 245 IDs below the age of 35, with 20 being even less than 25! On the other hand, a very high 3,033 individuals or 480 per cent of the total IDs are above the age of 60, the typical retirement age. Significantly, of these, as many as 1,380 are above 70, as many as 199 are past 80 and 8 are even beyond 90! Are many of these fit enough, physically and mentally, for the onerous board positions?

Suggestions

The mindset of the person getting appointed as director must be of one to act without fear or favor. So Independent Directors must be appointed/nominated by a separate meeting of the minority shareholders, not representing the majority investors. A separate meeting of such minority shareholders must be conveyed prior to the AGM to nominate such independent directors and AGM should formally appoint such independent directors. Any vacancy of the Board seat between two AGMs may be filled in by other independent directors continuing on the Board like Additional Director.

To ensure that the independent directors spend adequate time, they must be compensated well. Mere sitting fees of Rs.20,000 is obviously not enough. Such fees can be capped based on profits of the company or can be a fixed sum. Moreover Independent Directors should not get any options. Having options, generally may affect their independent status.

Chairmen of the committees must be a rotating position. At least in three years, a new member must be appointed as chairman of Audit /Compensation committee. Such provision would help a board to get new and fresh views and also the liability of independent directors should be distinguished from the executive directors and non-independent directors.

For securing the independence of independent director there is need to break the nexus between the independent directors and promoters who sponsor them, for that nomination of independent director must be done by SEBI and government. A company should have a clearly laid out policy where there should be specified role played by him at board, their tenure and age limit, qualification required etc. The focus must be on the quality of person who is going to be appointed. Selection of independent directors by SEBI and government would be fair and bring transparency in the selection procedure as well as can secure their independence to some extent. So far as age limit is concerned which must be review, minor should not be considered eligible for the chair of independent director; the minimum age limit for an independent director must be between 30-35. Company must clearly laid down qualification and experience required for the post of independent director in the policy. The appointed director must be rotated periodically to ensure the transparency and fairness in their decision. Legal protection must be provided to independent directors so that they can raise their voice against the management and force their views in the interest of shareholders.

If independent director does not fulfill their duty as a watchdog then it would amount to committing an offence. As Supreme Court in *Municipality of Bhiwandi & Nizampur* vs. *Kailas Sizing Works* has observed that the authority is not acting honestly where an authority has a suspicion that there is something wrong and does not make further enquiries.

In any case, the functional heads would be more loyal to their employer (promoter) than to the ID. Moreover, the functional heads could be suitably tutored by the promoters. IDs are being suggested to meet independently with the functional heads to get into depth as also to obtain varied perspectives. However, in reality, when most IDs do not even have the time to attend the board and committee meetings, how will they find time to talk independently with the management team? Moreover, they would not like to be seen as intruders. In any case, the poor knowledge base of most IDs would make them incompetent to ask the right questions from the management team.

It is true that many IDs have served on the boards for too long. Data shows that as many as 2,960 ID positions have been held for more than 6 years, out of which as many as 1,974 are for more than 9 years. However, this argument is faulty and assumes that IDs do not connive with the promoters in the first 6 or 9 years. The problem is that familiarity has existed even before their appointment. Fixed tenure could have been valid in case an outsider, not known to the promoter, came on to the board as with the passage of time, there is a possibility that he could become friendly with the promoter. The fixed tenure proposition has some value only in case we can ensure that independence was ensured at the time of appointment. Corporate governance is very subjective and cannot be measured through check boxes. Credit rating agencies, at best, can look at some visible aspects of CG—the quality of board members, their company/ industry knowledge, the attendance records, quality of agenda items, minutes of the meetings, and other boardroom practices, but this is all about the letter and not the spirit. CG rating was introduced in India almost 5 years ago on a voluntary basis. Only 19 companies opted for the same, and that too in the initial period. Since neither the companies nor the market has found value in CG ratings, this concept has been relegated to the shelves. It would be inappropriate in case CG rating is now made mandatory.

Another suggestion demands a budget for the IDs which they can use to hire the services of outside experts like lawyers, accountants and consultants. However, since the funds would be provided by the company, there could be a conflict of interest. But more fundamentally, would the IDs, who have been appointed by the promoters, be interested or even dare to take the promoters' intentions for an outside opinion? Some are suggesting that the IDs should meet independent of the promoters. Are they supposed to conspire in private against the promoters? What purpose would this serve given the truth that these people are really not independent? In any case, the hollow knowledge base of most IDs would make such meetings meaningless.

A few people are suggesting that presently most IDs are from the field of finance, and they should actually be from diverse fields like finance, law, academics, humanities etc. The issue again is the dilution of the meaning of IDs. Is their primary role bringing value to the company or is it protection of minority shareholders. If value indeed is the requirement, then hire professionals, and not IDs. New noises are being heard about the need for legal immunity to

IDs. Clearly, IDs want only the upside-fee, commissions, ESOPs and the perquisites, but not any downside. Undoubtedly, IDs should not be responsible for every wrong in a company as they have no control over or knowledge of it. In case they are, we will only see a further exodus of IDs, at least of the value directors. However, the IDs need to be accountable for decisions that they were a party to, with negligence being also treated as connivance. The mandatory requirement of ID should be scrapped, because IDs would always be insiders. On the other hand, corporates would neither accept outsiders nor should outsiders be imposed upon them. So the institution of IDs would always remain a farce, despite any number of loopholes that are plugged. Neither principle-based nor rule-based regulations will work.There is already a huge amount of information that corporates have to disclose. The need is to review these requirements; the focus should be on quality and not quantity, and in making them meaningful for the investors. While the disclosure requirements for initial listing are very elaborate, the continuing disclosure regime is very weak and needs to be overhauled. Finally, severe punishment for non-disclosure should be mandated. Instead of depending upon the IDs, the regulatory agencies should strengthen their surveillance and enforcement functions to ensure compliance of all laws and regulations. Alongside, there is a need to develop a system for swift and adequate punishment to the offenders, which will also act as a deterrent.

It would politically be a controversial move to scrap the very institution of ID, as it has been invoked for the protection of minority shareholders. Moreover, it is now a universally acclaimed regulation. It would also require admission of having introduced a bad practice in the first place, as if without proper thought. So it appears to me that, despite its ineffectiveness, ID would stay as an institution. If that be so and if IDs are indeed expected to play their defined role, the way forward is to at least strengthen the entire system surrounding their appointment and functioning.

One-third of the board should be of promoter-directors. Another one-third should be of value directors, appointed by the management, who would not be deemed as IDs. The balance one-third should be the real ID, who are necessarily qualified and have experience in corporate affairs, are picked up by the companies from a pool created by the regulator, and who are then subsequently trained and have a certification in directorship. If an auditor has to be compulsorily a member of ICAI, the people who are supposed to oversee, among others, the auditors themselves, should also have the requisite qualifications and be a member of an appropriate body. IDs can be brought in from outside as long as the process is transparent and fair.

It may be reiterated that there cannot be IDs if they are going to be appointed by the owners. Moreover, if quality cannot be mandated, corporates would continue to comply only in letter and would keep finding new loopholes when the present ones are plugged. Yet, some progress can be made by implementing the following suggestions.

(a) The term 'relatives' needs to be expanded, to include relatives from the mother's side as well as wife's side and, in fact, cover more relatives.

(b) If IDs in a company are related to each other, only one of them should be deemed as an ID. SEBI, however, has prescribed only disclosures about the relationships, but would continue to deem these as IDs.

(c) The directors nominated by any outsider under a lenders' or a shareholders' agreement should not be treated as IDs. These are typically "persons acting in concert".

(d) SEBI has, upon my representation, issued only a non-mandatory guideline stating companies should ensure that the IDs should have the requisite qualifications and experience. This is too subjective. Some minimum qualifications and/or experience norms should be mandated.

(e) In addition, there is a need to mandate, at the least, a certificate course for IDs.

(f) The minimum age for IDs should be 35 years, at the least, and the maximum age should be capped at 65 years. If most jobs face retirement at 58 or 60 or 65, there is logic to it. Physically old and mentally tired people cannot be expected to be vigilant (in fact, they are likely to often go off to sleep during the board meetings).

(g) No person, including retired people, should be allowed to hold independent directorships in more than three listed companies. This number should be brought down to only one for persons who are also promoters of listed companies or who are full-time employees anywhere, as they have an existing huge responsibility on hand.

(h) Many of such meetings last but a few minutes. It may be worthwhile for recording and reporting of the start/end time of all board/committee meetings.

(i) A cap on remuneration may not be desirable, and should be left to each case. However, remuneration earned by an ID from any single company should not exceed 15 per cent of his total annual income, in order to reduce his dependence. ESOPs and commissions should not be granted to IDs. Incidentally, sharing of profits is banned in many countries, including the US and UK.

(j) Clause 49 presently requires all domestic subsidiary companies of a listed company to also have IDs. This requirement should be extended to foreign unlisted subsidiaries of the Indian listed companies.

(k) The promoters/management should prepare, for each board agenda item, an impact analysis on minority shareholders. This would help draw specific attention of the IDs to any issues that unduly enrich the promoters or are against the interests of the non-promoter shareholders.

(i) Non-compliance of Clause 49 needs to be punished. Putting up the names on the stock exchange websites is no punishment. Delisting the company works against the minority shareholders and in fact may encourage many companies to get delisted easily through this route. Suspension again harms the investors so does a penalty on the company. The only effective punishment is a significant fine on the promoters/managements in their personal capacities.

(m) There has been a spate of resignations of IDs in the recent times. Most would have cited personal or health pre-occupation as the reasons. The regulator should find a way to convert these IDs into whistle blowers of sorts, and identify the ills affecting the companies from which they have resigned.

(n) Institutions would have to shed their passive, inactive roles and take proactive decisions on company agendas. They should also be required to publicly disclose annually all negative stances that they have taken. Greater institutional investors' involvement shall also keep the IDs on their toes. Institutional investors would also need to play an active role in appointment of IDs. Unless institutional investors attend AGMs and reject bad IDs, shareholders' endorsement shall remain a farce.

(o) An effective whistle blower policy needs to be mandated for each listed company. Anonymous complaints should also be entertained.

(p) The Satyam fiasco has clearly shown the CG awards in very poor light. Since such awards are very subjective and based on optical items, these do not capture the essence of CG. Contrary to expectations, these may create wrong impressions on the investors.

(q) Suggestions have been made that IDs should be elected by the non-promoter shareholders. This is fraught with unimaginable negatives. A suggestion has also been made that the promoters should instead create a panel and the minority shareholders should vote their choice. However, the panel would still be made only by the promoters and as such would still include names of only insiders.

(r) Suggestions have been made that IDs should be appointed by the government or SEBI. This idea should be discarded in the bud itself; this would lead to nepotism, corruption and unnecessary political interference. A good example of this practice can be seen in the quality of several IDs that have been appointed to the boards of PSUs.

So an independent director cannot escape from his liability. They will be held liable equally if they will not take any action against the wrong committed in his knowledge.

Conclusion

IDs have their origin in the monitoring role to the management and they found prominent place in the CG books with passage of time. They have found entry into statue books of company law of the developed world long before as basis for sound governance and as a check on management to curb any corporate fraud. In India, IDs entered into corporate lexicon via Clause 49 of Listing Agreement, based on recommendations of Birla Committee of SEBI. Chandra and Murthy Committee Reports further strengthened the role of IDs. MCA, after much of the effort has been successful to introduce the concept of ID in Indian statue books via Companies Bill, 2009. The first objective of this bill stipulates: "to segregate substantive law from the procedures to enable a clear framework for good CG that addresses the concerns of all stakeholders equitably". However, it seems that objective is given only in letter but not in spirits. In India, we have just imported the concept of IDs from developed world. We just prefer form over substance and structure over process. The concept developed abroad needs to be validated in home conditions, to be work successfully. SEBI tried to impose conditions of IDs over companies, but it has not worked very well in Indian conditions, companies have adopted it only in form but problem has remained. The practice has remained the alike. The problem of IDs lies mainly in the appointment process of ID and the present Bill does nothing new to change that.

The liability of the ID has substantially increased in the Bill and they are liable for financial and criminal penalties. Independent directors and executive directors were not adversaries, but were on the same side, and the Indian corporates would soon reach a stage where their internal systems would be stricter as compared to mandatory legal requirements, properly, for which certifying systems needed to be in place. Indian corporate governance, currently rated Asia's second best, would soon take the number one slot. Terming the concept of governance as being more misunderstood, one has to define it as "what adds value for the investor".

Moreover the company CEO's performance ought to be judged, and said the board was apt for this task. On how best to judge whether a company was into good corporate governance, "The truth lies somewhere between disclaimer and the disclosure." The corporates should be a step ahead of regulations and should ensure real compliance. Simplified and unambiguous regulations would encourage high standards of corporate governance. The independent director was the conscience keeper of the company. While consensus was needed, in the event that a situation would so require, an independent director should point out things in the interest of the company.

Satyam episode is proven to be tragic for the Indian corporate world, but it should be considered as a wake-up call to many. The Satyam case brought out the failure of the present corporate governance structure, in which independent directors failed to perform their responsibility effectively. As in Satyam case independent directors lacked commitment; they failed to live up to the stakeholders' expectations. The only way independent directors can stop wrong doing by acting collectively. It has demonstrated that even highly credible, qualified and educated persons are no insurance for corporate governance, that they are not independent of the promoters, providing blind support to them, and that they are no watchdogs of the minority shareholders whose interests they are supposed to serve.

There is no need to implement new laws; all we need to do is to renew existing laws. Independent directors may not be in a position to stop management fraud perpetrated at the highest level, but with high level of commitment and due diligence they should be able to identify signals that indicate that everything is not going right.

References

1. Anonymous (2009), *Independent Directors as Corporate watchdogs*, www.asclegal.com/asclegalpdf/CORPORATE_GOVERNANCE.pdf;
2. Birla Report (1999), 'Report of the Kumaramangalam Birla Committee on Corporate Governance', http://www.sebi.gov.in/commreport/corpgov.html
3. Bisht, M. S. (2009), 'Independent Directors—Are they really Independent?' on 12 October in caclub, www.caclubindia.com/articles/article_list_detail.asp?article_id...
4. Blue Ribbon Committee (1999), *Improving the Effectiveness of Corporate Audit Committees*, printed by the New York Stock Exchange and the National Association of Securities Dealers.
5. Cadbury Committee (1992), "The Financial Aspects of Corporate Governance (Cadbury Report)", Gee, London.
6. Chandra Report (2002), http://www.finmin.nic.in/downloads/reports/chandra.pdf
7. Chatterjee, D. (2009), "Independent Directors—An Indian Legal Perspective", available at papers.ssrn.com/sol3/.../SSRN_ID1335090_code1070093.pdf?
8. Companies Bill (2009), http://www.icsi.edu.in.
9. *Financial Express* (2006), January 10, 2006.

   Financial Reporting Council (2003), Higgs Report, , http://www.frc.org.uk
10. Financial Reporting Council (2005), "Smith Report", http://www.frc.org.uk
11. Financial Reporting Council (2008), "The Combined Code on Corporate Governance", June 2008.
12. Gordon, J. N. (2006), "Independent Directors and Stock Market Prices: The New Corporate Governance Paradigm", ECGI Law Working Paper No.74/2006, available at http://ssrn.com/abstract=928100.

13. Goswami, D. (2009), "Over-hyped Role of 'Independent Directors' in Corporate Governance Needs Re-look".

14. www.lawyersclubindia.com/articles/article-list_detail.asp?article_id

15. Haldea, P. (2009), "The naked truth about Independent Directors", www.directorsdatabase.com/IDs_Myth_PH.pdf

16. Hampel Report (1998), "Summary of Conclusions and Recommendations", Final Report, January, Gee, London.

17. Irani Committee (2005), Expert Committee on Company Law, Report of the Expert Committee to Advise the Government on the New Company Law, http://www.primedirectors.com/pdf/JJ%20Irani%20Report-MCA.pdf

18. Murthy Report (2003), "Report of the SEBI Committee on Corporate Governance", http://www.sebi.gov.in/commreport/corpgov.pdf

19. SEBI (2003), http://www.sebi.gov.in/commreport/cclause49.html

20. Sinha, R. N. (2002), "Should 'officer in default' cover independent directors also?"

21. Singh, J.P. and N. Kumar (2009), "Corporate Governance: The Contemporary Scenario", Converge of Corporate Governance Norms: Monograph, Cygnus Publication.

22. Shaun, J. M. (2007), "Hostile Takeovers in India: New Prospects, Challenge, and Regulatory Opportunities", vol. (3), COLOM. BUS. L. REV. 800.

23. Treasury Committee, House of Commons (2009), "Banking Crisis: Reforming Corporate Governance and Pay in the City", Ninth Report of Session 2008–09.

24. Verma, S. K. and S. Gupta (2004), "Corporate Governance and Corporate Law Reform in India", IDE Asian Law Series No. 25, Institute of Developing Economies (Ide-Jetro), Japan.

Corporate Governance Agenda of New Millennium
With Special Reference to Banking Sector

Dr. Jagannath B. kukkudi
Prof. Nagaratna M. Chowdhary

ABSTRACT

Governance is that separate process or certain part of management or leadership processes that make decisions that define expectations, grant power, or verify performance. Corporate Governance is the relationship among various participants in determining the direction and performance of companies. The primary participants are Shareholders, Management and the Board of Directors. Other participants including the employees, customers, suppliers, creditors and community. The concept of Corporate Governance has gained tremendous importance in the recent past, especially in India, after the second half of 1996.

The banking sector is not necessarily totally corporate. Some part of it is, of course, but a segment of banks is mostly government owned as statutory corporations or run as cooperatives–just like your bank. Banking as a sector has been unique and the interests of other stakeholders appear more important to it than in the case of non-banking and non-finance organizations. In the case of traditional manufacturing corporations, the issue has been that of safeguarding and maximizing the shareholders' value. In the case of banking, the risk involved for depositors and the possibility of contagion assumes greater importance than that of consumers of manufactured products. Further, the involvement of government is discernibly higher in banks due to importance of stability of financial system and the larger interests of the public.

Introduction

Corporate Governance is the relationship among various participants in determining the direction and performance of companies. The primary participants are Shareholders, Management and the Board of Directors. Other participants including the employees, customers, suppliers, creditors and community. It can be defined as the set of systems and process, which ensure that a company is managed to the best of interests of all the shareholders. The concept of Corporate Governance has gained tremendous importance in the recent past, especially in India, after the second half of 1996.

The banking sector is not necessarily totally corporate. Some part of it is, of course, but a segment of banks is mostly government owned as statutory corporations or run as cooperatives—just like your bank. Banking as a sector has been unique and the interests of other stakeholders appear more important to it than in the case of non-banking and non-finance organisations. In the case of traditional manufacturing corporations, the issue has been that of safeguarding and maximising the shareholders' value. In the case of banking, the risk involved for depositors and the possibility of contagion assumes greater importance than that of consumers of manufactured products. Further, the involvement of government is discernibly higher in banks due to importance of stability of financial system and the larger interests of the public. Since the market control is not sufficient to ensure proper governance in banks, the government does see reason in regulating and controlling the nature of activities, the structure of bonds, the ownership pattern, capital adequacy norms, liquidity ratios, etc.

Main Reason for the Upsurge of CG

The resent interest about Corporate Governance is primarily a product of four factors.

- Assertion of rights by the Shareholders.
- Significance presence of Foreign Institutional Investors.
- Awareness on the part of lending Institutions.
- Integration India in to the world Economy.
- Strong media presence.

Shareholders have not been able to fulfill the historic role effectively for the reason that they are widely spread and many of them find it difficult to travel to the meeting place. But in the context of complex nature of modern business, the scope of areas requiring shareholder's approval has enlarged. The significant presence of foreign institutional investors who demand greater professionalism in the management of Indian corporate has also led to the keen interest in the Corporate Governance.

There is awareness on the part of lending institutions, which are now being subjected to rigorous accounting norms, particularly with regard to income rendition and provisions against non-performing loans so they are giving much more emphasis to good and efficient Corporate Governance. There is the integration of India into the world economy, which depends that Indian industry should pay the game by a standard set of international rules rather than continue their anachronistic practices.

Dr. Rao (1999) considers that following issue are important in Corporate Governance:

- Sound Management
- Fiduciary relationship
- Return on Integrity
- Responsibility and Accountability

Evolution of Corporate Governance Draft Code

The United Nations Committee on Transnational Corporation sponsored a study on the responsibility of parent company for their subsidiaries. It evolved a code, which is a comprehensive one and touches upon general, economic, political as well as financial and social issues.

Boardroom Practices in India, 1989

A study titled Boardroom Practices in India was conducted by Dr. C.L. Bansal in 1989 to examine the structure, composition and functioning pattern of Corporate Boards of 100 Corporate Leaders by the process of historical evolution of Board Management System in India. The major findings of the study were the shift from the family boards to the professional boards and also most of the findings are similar to that of the Cadbury Report of 1982.

Cadbury Committee UK, 1991

In UK, in May 1991 the Financial Reporting Council, the London Stock Exchange and the Accountancy Profession to study and examine the financial aspects of Corporate Governance set up a Committee under the Chairmanship of Sir Adrian Cadbury, jointly. The Report submitted by the committee on December 1, 1992 aims at bringing greater clarity to the respective responsibilities of directors, shareholders and auditors and to strengthen trust in the corporate system.

Greenburry Committee UK

A study group on directors' remuneration was formed under Sir Richard Greenbury at the initiative of the Confederation of British Industry, while Cadbury Committee dealt with board matters of governance in relation to companies, Greenbury Committee dealt solely with director's pay.

Corporate Governance and Corporate Management

Corporate Governance is different from Corporate Management. A corporation being a juristic person cannot function itself and the persona of a company manifests itself through the Board of Directors. Therefore the cause of Corporate Governance is better served depending upon how well the Board is constituted. In a sense, the quality of corporate Governance is the quality of the board itself.

Managers		*Directors*	
Doers	Take decision and manage within a framework	*Thinkers*	Watch, assess and establish framework
Short term	The horizon is the next task	*Long term*	Need to plan ahead
Subjective	Life entwined with the Corporate	*Objective*	Keep an independent perspective
Rational	Trained to think about problems	*Intuitive*	Emphasis to build relationships
Focuses	Concentrate on departmental issues	*Diffused*	Havemulti/dimensional responsibilities
Specialist	Operate in particular discipline	*Generalist*	Have a holistic perspective

Major Players in Corporate Governance

The major players in the area of Corporate Governance are the Boards, Shareholders and Employees. Externally the government, customers, lenders of money etc set the pace of Corporate Governance. In essence, Corporate Governance is the system by which the companies are directed and controlled. The Board of Directors are responsible for the governance of their enterprises. The shareholder's role in governance is to appoint the directors and the auditors. Therefore the role of the Board and of the shareholders is inter-active in nature and the quality of governance depends upon the level of interface established by them.

Role of the Board

The quality of the Board depends upon a number of factors like size of the board, its composition, proportion of whole time, part-time directors, chairman of the Board, role of nominee directors etc. These are the board parameters with reference to which the quality of contribution to the overall corporate governance can be judged. The Companies Act, 1956 provide the legal framework for the functioning of corporate boards. Inter alia, the Act envisages an interactive role between the corporate boards and their shareholders and also prescribes disclosure of financial and other information to the shareholders through the Annual Financial Statements.

Role of Shareholders

The Companies Act have recognized the supremacy of shareholders. It gives authority to shareholders to direct, control, conduct and manages the business and affairs of the Company. The Act has armed the shareholders with very effective and powerful weapons so as to ensure that the business and affairs of the company are properly managed. Enlarging the scope of areas requiring shareholder's approval, strengthening the role of proxies, introducing postal ballot system, right to initiate matters for inclusion in the agenda of general meetings, need to prescribe a higher number of shareholders including those represented by the proxies for the purpose of forming quorum and the need to educate the shareholders on interpreting the financial statements, etc., would enhance shareholder's democracy and contribute to the overall improvement in the quality of corporate governance.

Role of Financial Institutions

Financial institutions by deputing their employees as nominee directors to companies to which financial assistance has been granted have brought in some measure of discipline and objectivity in the decision-making process, since they are not able to act independently in regard to the decision making process. They have to follow a 19 point formula devised by FIs regarding the corporate meetings.

Role of the State

Several legislations have been passed which set the minimum level of governance by the corporate and there is no maximum level of governance. Those who have achieved the minimum level of governance are better poised to achieve better governance. Now the state intervention has been reduced to the barest minimum, which indicates that the government has reposed confidence in the corporate in their ability to manage their affairs in the larger interest of our economy. This casts a larger responsibility on the corporate, which has to reflect in better corporate governance.

Code of Corporate Governance

Next issue that confronts the board is relating to priority. Should the board have first priority towards social issues or organizational issue or interest group issues? The members of board of directors who are nominees certainly take stance considering the interests of their nominators. However, what about other members. The board creates the vision, policies, and future directions of an organization. The board should arrive at a consensus relating to its key priorities and vision. A general belief is that "Board must maximize shareholder value with integrity and transparency"–claims K.B. Daadiseth (in the capacity of Chairman, HLL).

Fixing priority relating to values interests etc., is not enough. Code of Corporate Governance is required to guide board of directors and to ensure ethical practices. Many bodies have given Codes of Corporate Governance. We discuss here some important codes/guidelines:

CII CODE

- The full board, which should be single tired, should meet at intervals of two months, and at least six times a year.
- The non-executive directors should comprise at least 30 per cent of the board if one of them is a chairman.
- The non-executive directors comprise at least 50 per cent of the board if the chairman and the managing director is the same person.
- No individual should be a director on the boards of more than 10 companies at any given time.

- Non-executive directors should be active have defined responsibilities and be conversant with P & L accounts.
- Non-executive directors should be paid commissions for their professional inputs besides their sitting fees.
- Directors, who have not been present for at least 50 per cent of board meetings, should not be re-appointed.
- The board should be informed of operating plans and budgets, long-term plans, quarterly divisional results, and internal audit reports.
- Details of defaults, payments for intangibles, foreign exchange exposure and managers remuneration should be reported to the board.
- And audit committee comprising at least three non-executive directors, should be setup and given access to all financial information.
- Data should be provided in the annual report on monthly average share prices, value-added, and the financial performance of divisions.
- Disclosure norms and levels followed at home should be the same as those required for GDR issues.
- In case multiple credit ratings are obtained, all the ratings should be disclosed with comparisons explaining their significance.

Corporate India needs to make great steps in order to take the full advantage of globalization and information technology. The leadership of the centre comprising of board of directors and top management would have to be truly professional and responsible. There should be Code of Corporate Governance. There should be ethical practices. The centre should focus more on their core activities like giving direction, vision, empowering others. Business bodies like CII, FICCI etc, should form a consensus on arriving at a code of corporate governance and ethical practices. These practices should ensure protection on interest of shareholders, relationship management with stakeholders and social responsibilities.

Financial institutions should insist on professionalization and sound corporate governance for providing financial support to any organization. The rating agencies should give specific attention on Corporate Governance. There is some responsibility on every stakeholder to look at the Corporate Governance. The movement for better Corporate Governance is not just for the lending institutions or for investor protection, but, it is a movement for survival and growth of corporate in the era of globalization and liberalization.

Relevance of Corporate Governance to Indian Context

There is a need to bring better Corporate Governance in India in the context of liberalization, privatization and globalization (LPG) of Indian economy. The following factors underline the relevance of Corporate Governance to Indian context:

(i) Indian Boards are not in tune with times.

(ii) Holders of limited stake determine the destiny of major shareholders.

(iii) Family feuds result in stalemate and confusion.

(iv) Changing business environment.

(v) Shift in Government attitude.

(vi) Vision development.

(vii) Brand building.

(viii) Competitive edge.

(ix) Professional managers and independent auditors did not help much Emerging Issues in Management.

Measures taken by Banks towards Implementation of Best Practices

Prudential norms in terms of income recognition, asset classification, and capital adequacy have been well assimilated by the Indian banking system. In keeping with the international best practice, starting 31st March 2004, banks have adopted 90 days norm for classification of NPAs. Also, norms governing provisioning requirements in respect of doubtful assets have been made more stringent in a phased manner. Beginning 2005, banks will be required to set aside capital charge for market risk on their trading portfolio of government investments, which was earlier virtually exempt from market risk requirement.

Capital Adequacy: All the Indian banks barring one today are well above the stipulated benchmark of 9 per cent and remain in a state of preparedness to achieve the best standards of CRAR as soon as the new Basel 2 norms are made operational. In fact, as of 31st March 2004, banking system as a whole had a CRAR close to 13 per cent.

On the Income Recognition Front: There is complete uniformity now in the banking industry and the system therefore ensures responsibility and accountability on the part of the management in proper accounting of income as well as loan impairment.

ALM and Risk Management Practices: At the initiative of the regulators, banks were quickly required to address the need for Asset Liability Management followed by risk management practices. Both these are critical areas for an effective oversight by the Board and the senior management which are implemented by the Indian banking system on a tight time frame and the implementation review by RBI. These steps have enabled banks to understand, measure and anticipate the impact of the interest rate risk and liquidity risk, which in deregulated environment is gaining importance.

Conclusion

In the years to come, the Indian financial system will grow not only in size but also in complexity as the forces of competition gain further momentum and financial markets acquire greater depth. I can assure you that the policy environment will remain supportive of healthy growth and development with accent on more operational flexibility as well as greater prudential regulation and supervision. The real success of our financial sector reforms will however depend primarily on the organisational effectiveness of the banks, including cooperative banks, for which initiatives will have to come from the banks themselves. It is for the co-operative banks themselves to build on the synergy inherent in the cooperative structure and stand up for their unique qualities. With elements of good Corporate Governance, sound investment policy, appropriate internal control systems, better credit risk management, focus on newly-emerging business areas like micro finance, commitment to better customer service, adequate automation and proactive policies on house-keeping issues, co-operative banks will definitely be able to grapple with these challenges and convert them into opportunities.

References

1. Merger & Acquisition by Prof. V. K. Rao.
2. Study Material published by UPRTOU.
3. Study Material of M.Phil in Management published by Madurai Kamraj University.
4. Annual Report of Planning Commission of India, 2008-09.

10

An Analysis of Model/Mechanisms in Corporate Governance

Dr. Aravind, S.
Dr. Fisseha Girma Tessema
Dr. Hailay Gebretinsae

ABSTRACT

The societies of developed countries of the 21st century live in unprecedented prosperity. These nations have produced the highest standard of living for the most people in the history of the world. The concept of efficacy of the invisible hand led logically to a second notion that individuals attempts to pursue their separate interests, the intersections of their interests and objectives result in a natural state of competition. Specifically in the realm of business, we mean by this competition of raw materials, labor, customers and investment capital. This competitive environment leads to a "survival of fittest". While some people may fear this relentless ferreting out of the less efficient, it is perhaps the most energizing aspect of our system of free enterprise and competition. With the development of the economic system, enterprises of size and complexity not previously thought possible flourished. Without an effective system of governance, there would be chaos in organizations. It is the governance that brings order out of chaos. The issue of corporate governance continues to attract considerable national and international attention. This paper presents the mechanism/models of Corporate Governance of Organizations in various countries related to the activities of organizations that are conducted through structures that may lack transparency, or in jurisdictions that pose impediments to information flows and various other aspects that impedes the normal functioning of the organizations.

Keywords: Corporate Governance, Stakeholders, OECD, Economic System, California Public Employees' Retirement System (CalPers), Financial Crisis, etc.

Introduction

Corporate governance is typically perceived by academic literature as dealing with "problems that result from the separation of ownership and control". From this perspective, corporate governance would focus on: the internal structure and rules of the board of directors; the creation of independent audit committees; rules for disclosure of information to shareholders and creditors; and, control of management. A recent academic survey began with the following quote:

"Corporate governance deals with the ways in which suppliers of finance to corporations assure themselves of getting a return on their investment. How do the suppliers of finance get managers to return some of the profits to them? How do they make sure that managers do not steal the capital they supply or invest it in bad projects? How do suppliers of finance control managers?"

- From this point of view, corporate governance tends to focus on a simple model:
- Shareholders elect directors who represent them.
- Directors vote on key matters and adopt the majority decision.

- Decisions are made in a transparent manner so that shareholders and others can hold directors accountable.
- The company adopts accounting standards to generate the information necessary for directors, investors and other stakeholders to make decisions.

The company's policies and practices adhere to applicable national, state and local laws.

International Perspective on Corporate Governance

Over the last two decades a series of events have placed Corporate Governance issues as a top concern for both the international business community and the international financial institutions. Spectacular business failures such as the infamous BCCI scandal, the United States' savings and loan crisis, and the gap between executive compensation and corporate performance drove the demand for change in developed countries. More recently, several high profile scandals in Russia and the recent Asian crisis have brought corporate governance issues to the fore in the developing countries and transitional economies. Further, national business communities are learning and re-learning the lesson that there is no substitute for getting the basic business and management systems in place in order to be competitive internationally and to attract investment.

As a result, the World Bank, the Organization of Economic Cooperation and Development, most of the regional development banks, and the various national development agencies have either launched or expanded programs in this area in the last several years. Similarly, business-related organizations like the Center for International Private Enterprise, an affiliate of the US Chamber of Commerce, have placed corporate governance at the top of their list of concerns. Think tanks and business associations throughout the developing world and in the transitional economies are also focusing resources on these issues.

In developing countries, the roots of what is now recognized as corporate governance type issues can be found in the drive for privatization that grew in the late 1970s and throughout the 1980s. Clearly, creating a sound corporate structure should have been central to the success of privatization both from the point of view of the government seeking to sell the firm and from the point of view of the potential investors. In fact, some of the most telling failures in the early privatization experiences can be traced back to a lack of sound regulatory structures that allowed unwise business practices. Chile comes to mind in this respect. In the mid-1970s, Chilean business groups were able to purchase banks, often with only 20 per cent initial payments. In 1982, Chile experienced an economic crisis generated by a combination of external shocks and an overvalued exchange rate. The business groups responded by using their banks to shore up the firms which led both into even more serious trouble. Finally, the government responded by re-nationalizing a host of firms and banks.

The fall of the Berlin Wall and the drive to rapidly privatize the entire business structure of the post-communist economies began to increase interest in corporate governance as a development topic. As a start, state owned firms had to be corporative, i.e. converted from a governmental type structure to a corporate form. Second, the whole body of commercial law had to be put into place including bankruptcy, laws on property, accounting systems, and a host of other rules of the game. Most dauntingly, talent had to be nurtured. Few individuals had any experience as members of a board of directors.

It is perhaps not surprising that the countries that rushed into large-scale privatization, especially the Czech Republic and Russia; have experienced large scale corporate governance failures including asset stripping and fraud. Hungary, which chose to sell its firms to international strategic investors, and Poland, which chose to delay privatization of large companies, have had better results. Today, however, all of the post-communist countries have to come to grips with the need to substantially improve corporate governance standards and practices.

The Asian financial crisis has now driven the process worldwide much further. One of the lessons learned out of the crisis is that weak or ineffective corporate governance procedures can create huge potential liabilities for both individual firms and, collectively, for society. In this sense, corporate governance failures can potentially be as devastating as any other large economic shock. As Mr. Chatu Mongol Sonakul, the Governor of the Bank of Thailand has observed that the corporate governance is at the very heart of the development of both a market economy and a democratic society. That view may be a bit of a surprise to those who think mainly of corporate governance as the issues of shareholder protection, management control, and the famous principal-agent problems of such concern to management and economic theorists. The focus of the study is the concept of corporate governance as a key feature of the market system of competitive enterprise. In addition, the study shows why corporate governance should also be of direct concern to those focusing on democratic development especially rule of law issues. Corporate governance ultimately depends upon public-private sector cooperation to achieve both goals—the creation of a competitive market system and the development of law-based democratic society.

These concerns are not limited to developing countries, even in the advanced industrial societies, there is a global trend toward strengthening corporate governance. In the United States, there is mounting concern over the "independence" of independent audits as witnessed in the recent publicity surrounding violations of rules prohibiting auditors to invest in companies that they audit. In all of these cases, the underlying concerns center on ways to accomplish the core values of corporate governance including transparency, accountability, and building value.

Focusing on these types of internal control processes is quite natural when the subject is corporate governance within the advanced market economies. Although there are considerable differences between the Anglo-American,

German, Japanese, and other systems, they all share the luxury of defining the subject of corporate governance within the context of functioning market systems and highly developed legal institutions.

When the subject of corporate governance arises in the context of transitional or developing countries, it involves a much wider range of issues. The recent Asian economic crisis, the continuing turmoil in Russia, and the recent experience of the Czech economy have combined to push the issue of corporate governance from the sidelines to center stage. In Asia, what began as a financial crisis is now viewed to be a crisis of corporate transparency involving relationships between government and business, between holders of debt and equity, and the legal remedies for bankruptcy and cronyism. Further the lack of adequate institutions in Russia have resulted in several highly publicized cases involving allegations of asset stripping, stock register manipulation, and fraud. The Czech Republic privatization program has demonstrated the weakness of the voucher method in the absence of sound corporate governance mechanisms since it resulted in a lack of corporate restructuring and a consequent decline in competitiveness.

Each of these issues poses grave challenges for both the functioning of a market economy and a democratic society. Solving corporate governance problems such as those listed above involves going beyond a narrow view of how owners and managers of capital interrelate. In developing or transitional economies, the standard definition should be supplemented by placing it in context as follows:

"Corporate governance systems depend upon a set of institutions (laws, regulations, contracts, and norms) that create self-governing firms as the central element of a competitive market economy. These institutions ensure that the internal corporate government procedures adopted by the firms are enforced and that management is responsible to owners (shareholders) and other stakeholders".

The key point in this context is that the public and private sectors have to work together to develop a set of rules that are binding on all and which establish the ways in which companies have to govern themselves.

Creating New Norms

Transitional economies have to make fundamental changes in the relationship between citizens and the state in order to create market economies. The clear understanding in a market-oriented society (i.e. non-statistic) is that all actions not forbidden by law are allowed. That expectation is at the heart of private, individual initiative. The converse rule has been applied in command economies and in economies with a statistic tradition. That is, only those actions specifically authorized by law, regulation, or written permission are allowed.

Building a market economy requires a complete overhaul of legal norms to allow for innovation and initiative rather than predefining areas of allowable activity. That is why corporate governance should be thought of as a mechanism for creating self-governing organizations. However, it is equally important to emphasize that a market economy is not simply the absence of governmental intervention.

How often has it been said that, "the government should get out of the way and let the market function". Of course, that idea is a myth. Government is absolutely essential in setting up the framework of a market economy. Without rules and structures of a binding nature, anarchy results. Under such conditions business becomes nothing but "casino capitalism" where investments are simply bets: bets that people will keep their word, bets that the firms are telling the truth, bets that employees will be paid, and bets that debts will be honored. What corporate governance is all about in larger terms is how a structure can be set up that allows for a considerable amount of freedom within the rule of law. Ultimately, these arrangements provide the basis for the establishment of trust, one of the most important ingredients in business.

Organization for Economic Co-operation and Development(OECD) Principles

A useful first step in creating or reforming the corporate governance system is to look at the principles laid out by the OECD and adopted by the governments which are members of the OCED itself. The OECD principles include the following elements:

The Rights of Shareholders

These include a set of rights including secure ownership of their shares, the right to full disclosure of information, voting rights, participation in decisions on sale or modification of corporate assets including mergers and new share issues. The guidelines go on to specify a host of other issues connected to the basic concern of protecting the value of the corporation.

The Equitable Treatment of Shareholders

Here the OECD is concerned with protecting minority shareholders rights by setting up systems that keep insiders, including managers and directors, from taking advantage of their roles. Insider trading, for example, is explicitly prohibited and directors should disclose any material interests regarding transactions.

The Role of Stakeholders in Corporate Governance

The OECD recognizes that there are other stakeholders in companies in addition to shareholders. Banks, bond-holders and workers, for example, are important stakeholders in the way in which companies perform and make decisions. The OECD guidelines lay out several general provisions for protecting stakeholder interests.

Disclosure and Transparency

The OECD also lays out a number of provisions for the disclosure and communication of key facts about the company ranging from financial details to governance structures including the board of directors and their remuneration. The guidelines also specify that annual audits should be performed by independent auditors in accordance with high quality standards.

The guidelines provide a great deal of detail about the functions of the board in protecting the company, its shareholders, and its stakeholders. These include concerns about corporate strategy, risk, executive compensation and performance, as well as accounting and reporting systems.

The OECD guidelines are somewhat general and both the Anglo-American system and the Continental European (or German) systems would be quite consistent with them. However, there is growing pressure to put more enforcement mechanisms into those guidelines. The challenge will be to do this in a way consistent with market-oriented procedures by creating self-enforcing procedures that do not impose large new costs on firms. The following are some ways to introduce more explicit standards:

- Countries should be required to establish independent share registries. All too often, newly privatized or partially privatized firms dilute stock or simply fail to register shares purchased through foreign direct investments.
- Standards for transparency and reporting of the sales of underlying assets need to be spelled out along with enforcement mechanisms and procedures by which investors can seek to recover damages.
- The discussion of stakeholder participation in the OECD guidelines needs to be balanced by discussion of conflict of interest and insider trading issues. Standards or guidelines are needed in both areas.
- Property rights.
- Internationally accepted accounting standards should be explicitly required and national standards should be brought into alignment with international standards.

Internal company audit functions and the inclusion of outside directors on audit committees' needs to be made explicit. The best practice would be to require that only outside, independent directors be allowed to serve on audit committees. A good example of model corporate governance procedures that builds on many of these points is the General Motors guidelines which are frequently used as a Code of Corporate Governance by others. Interestingly, the pension funds have also become a major source of improved corporate governance along the same lines. Specifically, the California Public Employees' Retirement System (CalPers) has developed a very active program to promote good corporate governance and they, along with other pension funds, are using their investment clout to force change. CalPers' has taken this approach in order to increase the returns on their investments by ensuring that the firms are well run and that corporate strategies are well thought out. As more and more pension fund investments flow into developing countries, these funds can be expected to make similar demands in these countries.

Some may think that these standards are too heavily influenced by the Anglo-American tradition and are not really necessary in most countries. A recent study by the Center for European Policy Studies noted that the wider the distribution of shareholding, the greater is the role of the market in the exercise of corporate control. Hence there is more need for corporate governance procedures in this type of economy than in one where shareholding is relatively concentrated. The report went on to note, however, that financial market liberalization, increased privatization, and the growing use of funded systems to support pensions is driving European countries toward more explicit and more comprehensive rules on corporate governance. In short, globalization is forcing convergence of different systems into a more open and internationally accepted set of standards.

The reason why it is important to take note of the trends toward convergence is that many people have cited the European experience as proof that corporate governance issues only apply to countries that follow an Anglo-American tradition, such as India, for instance. Recent history would seem to show that, without sound corporate governance procedures, including the larger institutional features mentioned earlier, economic crises in developing countries are likely to become more frequent. Many developing countries face rather stark choices: create the type of governance procedures needed to participate in and take advantage of globalization, run the risk of severe (and frequent) economic crises, or seek to build defensive walls around the economy. It should be noted that the last option usually entails the risk of keeping out investors, new technologies, and lowers growth rates dramatically.

Another consideration in the debate over corporate governance systems is the risk that individual firms face. Unless a company is able to build the kinds of governance mechanisms that attract capital and technology they run the risk of simply becoming suppliers and vendors to the global multinationals.

Benefits to Society

A strong system of corporate governance can be a major benefit to society. Even in countries where most firms are not actively traded on stock markets, adopting standards for transparency in dealing with investors and creditors is a major benefit to all in that it helps to prevent systemic banking crises. Taking the next step and adopting bankruptcy procedures also helps to ensure that there are methods for dealing with business failures that are fair to all stakeholders, including workers as well as owners and creditors. Without adequate bankruptcy procedures, especially enforcement systems, there is little to prevent insiders from stripping the remaining value out of an insolvent firm to their own benefit.

Recent research has also shown that countries with stronger corporate governance protections for minority shareholders also have much larger and more liquid capital markets. Comparisons of countries that base their laws on different legal traditions show that those with weak systems tend to result in most companies being controlled by dominant investors rather than a widely dispersed ownership structure. Hence, for countries those are trying to attract small investors—whether domestic or foreign—corporate governance matters a great deal in getting the hard currency out of potential investors' mattresses and floorboards.

Many economists and management experts make the point that competition in product markets and competition for capital act as constraints on corporate behavior, in effect forcing good corporate governance. The fact that pension funds such as CalPers have had to take a very active role in improving corporate governance would seem to contradict this point. However, whether or not this is really the case in developed market economies, competition is surely a much smaller factor in transitional and developing countries. In many developing countries, competition in product or goods markets is quite limited, especially where significant regulatory barriers exist. These realities further underscore the importance of adopting the best possible corporate governance systems in countries where the market system is underdeveloped.

Corporate governance is also directly related to another topic that has emerged to a position of great prominence world wide – combating corruption. In many societies this is not a subject that is easy to deal with, both because of political sensitivities as well as potential legal action. Yet corruption has to be dealt with in order to secure a position in the global economy and to secure the benefits of economic growth. The recent signing of the OECD anti-bribery convention is the beginning, not the end, of a concerted global anti-corruption campaign. Efforts to improve corporate governance, especially in the provision of transparency in corporate transactions, in accounting and auditing procedures, in purchasing, and in all of the myriad individual business transactions is a large scale effort. Nevertheless, strengthening the corporate governance standards along lines suggested above would be one place to start.

Improving corporate governance procedures can also improve the management of the firm, especially in areas such as setting company strategy, ensuring that mergers and acquisitions are undertaken for sound business reasons, and that compensation systems reflect performance. It is also important to note that good corporate governance systems also have to include improvements in management systems. In many developing countries, there has been a tradition of very centralized management usually involving the owners of the firms directly. Throughout Latin America, for example, the family business groups have tended to dominate the business landscape. This is now changing rapidly as a result of financial globalization, adherence to the World Trade Organization's liberalization rules, and the increasing integration of Latin America's regional markets. As a result, Latin America's firms are increasingly adopting modern management techniques, financial accounting systems, and business strategies. All of this requires delegation of authority, paying increased attention to developing highly trained staff, and use of management information systems in lieu of the older centralized decision-making structures. It is highly probable that these trends will force similar changes throughout the Middle East.

Conclusion

One way to sum up the concept of corporate governance is to look at it from the perspective of the corporate director. Increasingly directors are being held liable for their actions or inaction, at least in the developed countries. What then does a director need to be able to function and have a balanced view of the firm? According to one seasoned corporate director, the following is the minimum essential information:

- Operating systems, balance sheets, and cash flow statements that compare current period and year-to-date performance to target performance and previous year performance.
- Management comments about current performance that focuses on explaining the deviations from the target performance and revise performance targets for the remainder of the year.

- Information on the company's market share.
- Minutes of management committee meetings.
- Financial analysts' reports for the company and its major competitors.
- Employee attitude surveys.
- Customer preference surveys.
- Key media articles on the company, its major competitors, and industry trends.

The list not only sums up the key responsibilities of a board by showing the kinds of information that a board should review and disclose. These concerns reinforce the argument that corporate governance reflects the underlying systems of law and regulation. Most importantly, without sound and accurate accounting systems, how could the director function? The list also points up that good corporate governance will bring with it modern management systems. For example, reviewing the minutes of the management committee meetings implies that a functioning management committee system is in place with delegation of authority and accountability.

Investors, creditors, workers, and others also need such information. Unlike the corporate director, they do not have the time or resources to compile and analyze the information needed to make sound decisions. This is where the media, especially the financial media, comes into the picture. A vigorous and well informed journalist community is essential for the small investor and for the other stakeholders in society, including employees.

Creating sound system of corporate governance is a high priority for both the public and the private sectors. However, there may be a temptation for the private sector to just say, "well, we'll let the government work this out and then we'll follow the results." In some cases, there may also be a temptation—especially for the countries with protected markets and a large state sector—to put off corporate governance reform until after the privatization process and other types of reforms are fully completed. Experience would indicate that this would be a very unfortunate decision. Both the private and public sectors have much to gain by setting up clear and simple rules for all to follow. A sound corporate governance structure will be a great inducement to international trade and investment. In addition, sound corporate governance systems are a major advantage to those countries seeking to fight corruption. In this sense, good corporate governance is a way for the private sector to protect itself from outside demands and for the public sector to prevent undue influence in governmental decision-making.

However, it is vital to avoid simply copying other countries systems or asking foreign experts to write model laws. Although the foreign donor community often pushes this type of approach, it should be resisted. Throughout Central and Eastern Europe a network of extremely capable policy research institutes, think tanks, has been formed and others will surely follow. Many of these centers have been formed with the backing of the business leadership and are in a position to devise, adapt, and advocate for systems that will be appropriate to the status of each country. In the process, not only will the resulting policy reforms advance better systems of corporate governance, they will point to the need for other reforms. The need for adoption of modern management systems including areas such as knowledge management and strategic planning will become more apparent in the process. As more and more countries in the region enter the WTO process and further their participation in the global market, the demand for corporate governance will surely grow. It's up to the policy research centers, the national business associations, and others in civil society to work with governments to craft the best national systems.

References

1. *Corporate Governance* by John L. Colley, Jacqueline L. Doyle - Tata Mc-Graw Hill, New Delhi, 2009.www.cmie.com

2. www.oecd.org

3. www.corpgov.net
4. www.Corporate Governance.com
5. www.encycogov.com
6. Whatiscorpgov.asp
7. www.Corporate governance.Asp

Index

A

All India Management Association (AIMA), 17
- benefits to society, 189-191
- creating new norms, 185
- international perspective on corporate governance, 181-185
- introduction, 180-181
- organization for economic co-operation and development principles, 186-189

Analysis of model/mechanisms in corporate governance, 179-194
Aravind, S., 1
Asset Liability Management, 9
Associated Chamber of Commerce and Industry (ASSOCHAM), 4, 18

B

Bais, Santosh Singh, 128
Bank Nationalization Act, 48
Banking Regulation Act and Companies Act, 48
Basel Committee on Banking Supervision, 40
Basel II and CG, 40-42
Berlin Wall, 182
Bias, Santosh Singh, 1
Blue Ribbon Committee (1999), 51
Boardroom practices in India, 171

C

Cadbury code of best practices, 89
Cadbury committee UK, 1991, 171
Cadbury Report, 4
Chidambaram, P., 122
Chopra, Amarjit, 16
Chowdhary, Nagaratna M., 168
Code of Best Practices, 4
Committees of the board, 94
Companies Act, 1956, 138
Confederation of Indian Industries (CII), 4
Corporate Compliance Committee, 23
Corporate governance agenda of new millennium, 168-178
- boardroom practices in India, 1989, 171
- Cadbury committee UK, 1991, 171
- CII code, 174-176
- code of corporate governance, 174
- corporate governance and corporate management, 171-172

evolution of corporate governance draft code, 171
introduction, 169-170
main reason for the upsurge of CG, 170
major players in corporate governance, 172
measures taken by banks towards implementation of best practices, 176-177
relevance of corporate governance to Indian context, 176
role of financial institutions, 173
role of shareholders, 173
role of the board, 172-173
role of the state, 173-174
Corporate governance in bank, 33-44, 128-137
Basel II and CG, 40-42
challenges, 40
definition, 34-35
essential governance principles, 132-133
finding, 42-43
genesis of corporate governance, 131-132
genesis of corporate governance, 33-34
introduction, 34, 129
measures taken by banks towards implementation of best practices, 38-39, 133-134
measures taken by regulator towards corporate governance, 39-40
measures taken by regulator towards corporate governance, 134-135
need for corporate governancc in banks, 129-130
objective, 35-36
reasons for high degree of oversight, 130
role of board of directors and their committees, 37-38
role of the government and the regulator, 36-37
why corporate governance in bank, 35
Corporate governance in India, 15-32
independent directors, 21-22
auditors, 22-23
constitution of investor relations cell, 24-26
corporate compliance committee to be made mandatory, 24
corporate disclosure, 26-27
Director's responsibility statement to include statement on compliances, 24
limit on number of directorships, 22
preferential warrants, 27-28
risk management, 23
secretarial audit, 23
separation of roles of chairman and CEO, 22
Indian CG system after Satyam scam, 19-21
learning from Satyam scandal, 16-19
Corporate governance in Indian

financial institutions, 45-108
analysis of different parameters of corporate governance, 62-63
corporate governance
and co-operative bank, 59
and insurance companies, 59-60
and non-banking financial companies, 58-59
in Indian public financial institutions, 58
in search for a suitable definition, 48-50
on Indian perspectives, 51-55
on international perspectives, 50-51
introduction, 46-48
key observations, 69-71
objective of the study, 62.
policy framework of CG in Indian banking committee recommendations and implementation, 61-62
principles of corporate governance, 56-57
problems of corporate governance in banks in India, 60-61
significance of corporate governance, 55-56
Corporate Governance Voluntary Guidelines 2009, 20

D

Das, Sanjay Kanti, 45
Deed of Covenant, 8
Depositories Act, 1996, 51

E

EDIFAR (Electronic data Information Filing and Retrieval System), 27
Essential governance principles, 132-133

F

Finance by Indian banks, 120-121
Fit and proper criteria for directors of banks, 91

G

Ganguli, Ashok, 7
Ganguly Committee, 92
Gebretinsae, Hailay, 179
Genesis of corporate governance, 131-132
Global Corporate Governance Forum, 48
Greenburry Committee UK, 171

I

Indian Banking System, 10
Indian Banking System, 39
Institute of Chartered Accountants of India, 16
International Business School of Losan, 114
International Chamber of Commerce, 49
International Private Enterprise, 181

K

Kukkudi, Jagannath B., 168
Kumar Mangalam Birla Committee, 51

L

Legal framework, 118-119

Lehman Brothers, 16
Liberalization, privatization and globalization (LPG), 176
London Stock Exchange, 3

M

Mandatory recommendation, 104
Memorandum of Association (MoU), 25
Ministry of Corporate Affairs (MCA), 24
Mistry, Snehalkumar H., 116
MNC, 18
Mohanta, Giridhari, 116

N

NABARD, 67
Non-banking financial companies, 109-115
- highlights, 111
- introduction, 110-111
- present scenario, 111-112
- survival of fittest, 112-113

NPAs, 11

O

OECD Principles of Corporate Governance (1999), 51
Overseas deals, 126

P

Panigrahi, Ashok Kumar, 15
Peer Group Comparison, 12, 135
Policy framework of CG in Indian banking, 61-62
Prudential way of tapping global opportunities by Indian companies, 116-127
- introduction, 116-117
- factors behind the growth of Indian corporate on global front, 117-118
- liberalization of overseas investment policy, 118
- legal framework, 118-119
- funding, 118-120
- finance by Indian banks, 120-121
- modes for tapping the global opportunities merger, 121
- acquisition, 121-122
- emerging trend and its effect, 122-125
- overseas deals, 126

R

Ranoor, Srinivas, 128
Recommendations applicable only public sector banks, 95
Relating to the board of directors, 89
Reserve Bank of India, 7, 10
Reserve Bank of India Act, 48
Role of corporate governance in development of co-operative banks in India, 1-14
- genesis of corporate governance, 3-4
- introduction, 2-3
- special place of banking, 5
- reasons for high degree of oversight, 5-6
- role of the government and the regulator, 6-7
- board of director and their committees, 7-8
- measures taken by banks towards implementation of best practices, 8-10

ALM and risk management practices, 9
capital adequacy, 8
development of human capital, 10
income recognition front, 8
internal control systems, 9
professionalism, 9
prudential norms, 8
measures taken by regulator towards corporate governance, 10
investment ceiling, 12
off-site surveillance mechanism, 12
prompt corrective action, 12
transparency, 10-11
Role of independent directors in good corporate governance in India, 138-167
introduction, 139-140
definition and meaning, 140-141
objectives, 141-142
Indian scenario, 143-145
companies act and independent directors, 145
legal provisions, 145-146
independent directors under listing agreement in India, 146-147
independent directors in the light of the companies bill, 2009, 148-153
are independent directors independent in India, 153-154
drawbacks, 154-156
suggestions, 157-164

S

Satyam scam, 19-21
SBI Act, 48
SEBI, 23
Securities and Exchange Board of India (SEBI), 4
Shahani, Ranjit, 18

T

Tessema, Fisseha Girma, 179
Treadway Committee in USA, 50

U

United States, 28, 181

V

Vataliya, K.S., 109
Virparia, Vimla, 33
Vyas, H.D., 109

W

World Bank, 48, 181
WTO, 135

❑❑❑